MW01232176

The Light Of Home In The Western Dusk

How Worship Restores Us as a Person & People

Jerry M. Roper, Ph.D.

BookLocker
Trenton, Georgia

Print ISBN: 979-8-88531-065-9
Ebook ISBN: 979-8-88531-066-6

Published by BookLocker.com, Inc., Trenton, Georgia.

Printed on acid-free paper.

BookLocker.com, Inc.
2022

First Edition

Dedicated to the memory of my mother, Maris, my father, Hulert, and all the saints at Park Avenue Baptist Church in Atlanta, Georgia, who taught a young boy to love the Lord God,

and

Written for my granddaughters, Claire Elizabeth and Isla Catherine, and "for a future generation, that a people not yet created may praise the Lord." (Psalm 102:18)

Acknowledgements

A dash of salt, just the right herbs, and not overcooking — these are the things that transform a simple dish into a delightful dining experience, and that's exactly what my wife has done for this book; transform it. Her patience, keen eye, and sharp mind corrected mistakes, smoothed out rough spots, improved clarity, and moved the book to a higher, better plane. She is my partner for life, my best friend, and the light touch of her hand is felt on every page.

Dear friend, Minister of the Word in the truest Reformed tradition, beloved pastor, and shepherd to his flock, Rev. John W. Daniel, D. Min. is a brother in Christ, and because we share a love for college football and all things of the South, he counts as family. Importantly, John and I share a desire that the church fulfill what it should be and what it can be. His unflagging support, encouragement, and guidance was a force moving this book forward. At times, we collaborated on writing, and although he doesn't appear as an author, some of his words are likely in the text. What is certain, however, is that his ideas and spirit are present throughout the manuscript, and for that I thank him.

Writing is sometimes like wandering in the woods alone. You ask yourself, "Am I headed in the right direction?" Steve and Peggy's thoughtful commentary and sincere encouragement were welcomed markers along the wooded trail that told me I was on the right path.

"Bind us together in love." These hymnal words are given life in the Basics & Foundation Class of First Presbyterian Church in Orlando, Florida. The class watched video presentations of each chapter. Their comments and observations were like editor's notes guiding me to a more finished and polished book. Their kindness, sincerity, and genuine concern for one another are cords of love that binds this class together.

Table of Contents

Prologue

Manchester, England

I'm sure that like me you've watched countless murder mysteries on TV and in movies. Typically, a scrap of evidence or inconsistency in a suspect's story is presented early in the investigation. Perhaps, it's an alibi that's not airtight or a door that can only be locked from the inside. Whatever it is, at the time it seems insignificant, but later it turns out to be the clue that solves the entire mystery. This tried and true boilerplate is precisely how this book came to be written. A seemingly insignificant experience years ago is the piece that ties this book together.

Roughly, ten years ago I was traveling on business to England. I worked for an American chemical company, and had been at our offices and laboratories outside of London for several days, but I needed to make a side trip to Manchester. My company had recently purchased a small manufacturing plant in that city, and I needed to size up the plant and meet the employees, who now reported to me. So, midmorning one day, I caught a train to Manchester that arrived just in time for the evening rush hour.

Outside the train station, I hopped in a taxi, exited the station, and then inched along in heavy traffic. It was early spring and the long shadows of dusk were setting in, but there was still enough light that up ahead on a hilltop, I could see a lovely brownstone church. What caught my eye was that even from a distance it was clean and well maintained. There was not a trace of the dingy grime that typically covers old European churches. The true rich color and beauty of the brownstones were on full display. As my taxi got nearer, I could see that the stained-glass windows had recently been refurbished. The window frames were freshly painted and in the gathering twilight, the light inside the church shined through the stained glass as brilliant blues, crimsons, and golds. As I got closer still, the landscape lighting switched on. It was almost dark now, and the carefully placed lighting accentuated the beauty of the church and its manicured surroundings.

I thought what a wonderful church! I'd like to meet the minister and people of the congregation, because here was obviously a vibrant church, a living church, and a church that says to the world only the best for Our Lord and Savior, Jesus Christ. Still, the traffic crept along, and by the time my taxi was in front of the church dusk was giving way to night, but there was an illuminated sign. I would learn the name of this wonderful church. As I read the sign, my spirits sank. "LUXURY CONDOS FOR SALE. ONLY 1 LEFT. CALL TODAY!" It wasn't a church at all. It was only a building that used to be a church. My imagined vibrant and worshiping congregation was just that, imagined. The secular had purchased the sacred, not from a living but, a dying church.

Ten years later as I write this book, this seemingly insignificant experience on an otherwise mundane taxi ride in Manchester has been in my thoughts. Here is the clue that reveals the deep mystery of our times. Western civilization is in the grip of a moral and spiritual dusk that grows darker by the decade. Night approaches, and the people who live in the "church condos" I'm sure are very comfortable. The sign said "LUXURY CONDOS," and based on the pristine condition of the outside of the building, I don't doubt the claim. I trust that the condo owners are very happy in their new homes. But here's the rub: in pursuit of a comfortable, luxurious lifestyle, they have supplanted the building's original *raison d'etre* with a purpose of their own making. They haven't simply converted the sacred into the secular, but instead have gutted the sacred so that its insides are no longer recognizable. The condo owners are living in a shell of what once was. Their homes are in a structure that has been changed into something it was never intended it to be, and so it is with all of Western civilization.

Twenty-first Century Westerners are living in a shell of a civilization that was never intended to be. In the last century and continuing into this one, we have gutted the *raison d'etre* of our civilization which is Judeo-Christianity. We are quite comfortable in our lifestyle, and the shell of our civilization – our institutions, governments, justice system, liberty, concern for human rights and the environment – appears to be sturdy, like the brownstones of the Manchester church. But just as it's insides were gutted and redesigned, so too are the insides of Western civilization. With Judeo-Christianity year-by-year being removed from the West, the inside of our civilization is undergoing renovation for a new intended purpose.

The gutting of the old and repurposing it for the new is celebrated by the modern architects and designers of the West – the media, celebrities, universities, politicians, and Silicon Valley tycoons to name a few. But, this vision of the future comes at a very steep cost, which is the loss of our identity both as a person and a people. As the old Judeo-Christian architecture of the West is removed and carted out to the trash bin, we have trouble recognizing our societal home. Worse, we lose our home's foundational story, because we don't know our home's faith. In fact, we don't even believe there is a place for the old faith or for God. Is it any surprise then that we are confused? Is it any wonder that we lose our way in the growing moral and spiritual darkness? We have traded the light of Christ in the sanctuary for the light of a big screen TV in a living room, and exchanged the fellowship of faith for a loneliness of the soul.

Through the pages of this book, I want you to hop into the back of my Manchester taxi. As we inch along in traffic, I will tell you stories of our home. These are true stories of who we were, who we are, who we ought to be, and who we can be. This is very much a book of stories, each of which reveal an aspect of Western civilization's foundational story that is rooted in Judeo-Christianity. The clue that ties all these stories together is the one that seems unimportant and insignificant. It is the church sanctuary. My hope is that when you have finished reading this book that you will understand why I was heartbroken to see that the brownstone church was now condos. If you have that understanding, then I've done my job in writing this book.

Jerry Roper
November, 2021

Introduction

Western Sleepers

MIST- I don't believe the sleepers in the house know where they are.
SMOKE - If the day ever comes when they know who they are, they may know better where they are. But who they are is too much to believe - either for them or the onlooking world.
(Excerpted from "A Cabin In The Clearing," a poem by Robert Frost.)

"A Cabin In The Clearing" paints a tranquil early morning picture of an isolated cabin, with the rising sun barely peeking over the tree tops. As dawn's light pushes into the clearing, no light is seen in the cabin's window, leaving us to assume that those inside are still sleeping. From the chimney, we watch wispy white smoke from the night's fire lazily drift skyward. In the adjacent vegetable garden, rays warm the earth and awaken a sleeping mist that rises, but then seems to change its mind and hovers near the ground, shrouding the garden in a ghostly fog. In this quiet woodland clearing, Frost imagines a conversation between Smoke and Mist. Mist states, "I don't believe the sleepers in the house know where they are." Smoke agrees and replies, "If the day ever comes when they know who they are, they may know better where they are." And, so it is with us in America and indeed all Western nations.

We are 21st Century sleepers, slumbering yet awake enough to sense that the early morning quietness makes us uneasy, discontented, and perhaps a bit anxious. The anxiety is not even close to the handwringing acute kind. It's the nagging kind. It is a chronic melancholy sinking kind of feeling that something in life is eschew, out of place, and even lost. Mist and Smoke pick up on this feeling and identify the problem. We sleepers don't know who we are, or where are we. This insight is helpful, and the key to putting our finger on the source of our melancholy is Mist's observation that the sleepers don't know where they are. Where they are is home. The cabin in the clearing is their home yet, as Frost's poem, which is set in an earlier century, tells us in subsequent lines, the sleepers are not in sync with the surrounding woods, they are not at ease with the nearby Native Americans, and traveling preachers stop by to counsel them in their cabin, but none of this helps. The cabin in the clearing does not feel like their home, and neither does the West for 21st Century sleepers. Westerners today have ambiguous, and even negative, feelings about home.

We have dwelling places that we call home – single-family homes, townhomes, apartments, condos, lake homes, mountain homes, beach bungalows, and we even have motor homes. For most of us, these are very comfortable, and by the world's standards even luxurious. But what we don't have is a home in the fullest sense of the word. A place where we say, this is who I am, this is where I belong, and I share a story and destiny with the people who are around me. It is this last bit that is the core problem.

Families – and today these come in many descriptions – can be close, loving, and even live in the same house for decades, and in the same town for all their lives. For these rooted families the answer to who I am and belonging comes easy, but move to that last bit – sharing a story and destiny with the people in their neighborhood, their city, or even nation – and the answers do not come so quickly. Are we really with them, the people around us; the people in our towns and cities? And, are they really with us? These are broader community, societal, and nationhood questions, and they are important because no individual and no family lives in isolation. All are affected by the society around them. This is the home that we can't locate. Who are we as Westerners? Where are we, not geographically on the globe, but as a society, as a people? What do we believe about ourselves? What is our story? What is our faith or faiths? Where does our destiny lie? Borrowing Thomas Jefferson's words in the Declaration of Independence, what truths do Westerners hold to be self-evident in the 21st Century?

In our libertine, mobile, busy, entertaining, and prosperous Western lives, these questions are answered in a multitude of ways, and literally, the answers are all over the map in part, because the world, i.e., non-Western people from around the globe, now live in Western nations, bringing with them answers based on their indigenous culture and religion. But, a mix of different faiths, philosophies, and cultures is only a minor part of Western confusion about who we are and where we are. The extent of our confusion becomes clear by looking, not at the new things that immigrants bring with them, but by ancestral Westerners asking, what does Western civilization have to offer our newest arrivals? Can the West offer them anything more than a job and an improved lifestyle? If Westerners were tasked with the responsibility of standing on a stage before a large audience of newly arrived immigrants and articulating for them the truths that Western civilization holds to be self-evident, what would we say?

You see, we are tasked with this job, but we cannot complete it, because today there is nothing within Western society that says, here are the truths that we believe about ourselves, humanity, the sanctity of life, the soul, marriage, the universe – all the big questions of life. Buddhist nations, Hindu nations, Muslim nations, Confucian nations, even Marxist communist nations can all answer these questions, but Western Christian nations cannot. For every self-evident truth expressed by one person or group another will attack it, saying it's a lie. Therefore, there is only one thing that is self-evident in Western society. We are confused. Therefore, we choose to sleep. Sleeping, i.e., ignoring the problem, is a lot easier than trying to find answers. Yet there are certain times in the quiet stillness of an early morning, when we lie awake and eavesdrop on the conversation between Mist and Smoke, and wonder are they right? We have that sinking feeling that they are, and that we really don't know who we are and where we belong. The purpose of this book is to provide answers to these questions of home and identity.

The answers found in this book do not rely upon data, demographics, statistics, trends, or comparisons. Such information is useful for documenting who we were and how we have changed over the decades of the 20th and now 21st Centuries, but this is a well plowed field of research, and what typically emerges from these studies is a host of conjectures and conclusions that are backward looking. Such studies are like a doctor, who can document the symptoms of an illness, but cannot diagnose the underlying disease and certainly cannot prescribe a treatment. Therefore, this book offers a different approach to finding answers. One that affords a diagnosis and offers a prescription. This book identifies the nexus of Western civilization. The nexus is that one place where the West's history, governments, institutions, religion, charities, philosophy, thought, and even science intersect. All roads in Western civilization pass through this place, and that place is the church sanctuary. Who Westerners are and where we are is conveyed through the worship service in Christian churches.

The songs, symbols, stories, Holy Scripture, sermons, sacraments, and fellowship in Christian worship have touched every aspect of Western culture, because for two millennia, it shaped the West. Christian worship is the West's nexus and also its Rosetta Stone. It is where all things meet and are translated into a societal template that is coherent, uniform, satisfying, rational, moral, and hopeful. The societal template that emerged from worship gave expression to Judeo-Christian morals, ethics, and justice which formed the foundation of Western governments, institutions, freedoms, and philosophy. Therefore, faith-worship-institutions-justice system-society worked in concert, because all were based upon the same template.

What developed was a civilization that was coherent and understandable to citizens who worshiped the God of Judeo-Christianity. From God, who is Our Creator and Christ, our Savior, came the truths that Westerners declared to be self-evident. But, if citizens do not worship and do not have an understanding of Judeo-Christianity, then Western civilization is bewildering. We are like amnesiacs, whose shattered memory cannot recognize the nexus of our civilization. We see churches and cathedrals in our cities, but only admire their architecture. We celebrate national holidays that originated in the Christian church, and have no idea of the connection. All Western languages, not just English, are enriched by phrases and expressions that are biblical, e.g., we escaped "by the skin of our teeth" (Job 19:20), and we would never guess that these common expressions came from the Bible. In America curiously, the United States Congress has a chaplain, who opens each new congress with prayer yet children are prohibited from praying in school. For two thousand years, we never questioned that God "knit me together in my mother's womb," and that we are "fearfully and wonderfully made" (Psalm 139:13-14) Yet today we cannot agree when human life begins. Untethered and unable to decipher our civilization's nexus, is it any wonder that we don't know who we are or where we belong?

Our problem today is that we do not worship and no longer read the Bible. Study after study has documented that the majority of 21st Century Westerners do not participate in Christian worship, and the Bible is perhaps at best just another book on the shelf. Therefore, it's Catch-22. The answers that the West needs are in the church sanctuary and on the pages of scripture, but society says, don't go in and don't open that book. There are no worthwhile answers in either! A civilization so divorced and even resentful of its foundational story is homeless, and no different than a homeless person on the streets of Western cities, who wanders aimlessly muttering to themselves. This is the West today: wandering, aimless, and incoherent. Who are we? Where is our home? What is our story? What has happened to us?

These are the questions answered in the following chapters, and the questions are answered by doing precisely the opposite of what Western society advises. We will open the Bible. Each chapter begins with scripture that is explained and set in context. The scripture passage is then linked, amplified, and illustrated by taking the reader on a trip from 1st Century Jerusalem to a place where an important event in Western civilization occurred. First Century Jerusalem is the starting point, because by the end of that century, Jesus' earthly ministry was completed. He was resurrected, ascended, and Christianity was rapidly spreading across the Roman Empire. The events of 1st Century Jerusalem were the beginning of the West's modern foundational story, and to tell our story, the chapters are organized into three parts.

"Part I. Awakened To Who We Are" arouses Western sleepers by reminding us what we once believed, but now have forgotten. However, this is not enough. It's like sitting next to your grandmother as she flips through an old family photo album, and you feel a tinge of nostalgia that soon passes.

Westerners need to know our stories of who we were, what we believed, and why we are not those same people today. Each of the three chapters in Part I begin by affirming tenets of Christianity that we once believed, but now doubt. Importantly, these chapters expose the sources of our doubt and distrust. With this insight, we better know who we are, and can begin to understand who we ought to be, which is the subject of Part II.

"Part II. Worship Tells Who We Were and Who We Ought To Be" takes us inside a typical Christian worship service. From the Call to Worship to the Benediction, the eight chapters of Part II tell true stories of the modern West that illustrate each part of the worship liturgy. Presidents and prime ministers have prayed Pastoral Prayers. Existentialist writers such as Jean-Paul Sartre have unwittingly illustrated Confession of Sin & Assurance of Pardon. The stories of Part II connect scripture, story, meaning, purpose, faith, and hope to demonstrate who we were and who we ought to be. Having experienced the worship service, we can now begin the restoration of who we are as a person and a people, which is the topic of Part III.

The four chapters of "Part III. Restored To Who We Can Be" tell true stories that identify what we have lost and how recovery is possible. The chapters are: Love & Justice, Goodness & Knowledge, and Worship & Fellowship. These virtuous traits are hard to spot in the West, and Part III explains how they were lost and looks forward to the time they will return.

By reclaiming our foundational story, a new Western dawn awaits – a renaissance of the heart, mind, and soul of Western men and women. Amazingly, Smoke's answer to Mist hints at our awakening. Smoke says, "But who they are is too much to believe - either for them or the onlooking world." The message of Christianity is too much to believe. Yet, believe it for it is true! For two thousand years, the faith has illuminated the West, and by the light of Christ our civilization was built. When this generation of Westerners sees Christ's light and believes, then we will finally be at home. When the dawn of Christ's light comes, we will eavesdrop again on Smoke and Mist. They will say, "The sleepers are awake now. They know who they are, and where they are."

Part I:
Awakened To Who We Are

Q. 1. What is the chief end of man?
A. Man's chief end is to glorify God, and enjoy him forever.
The Westminster Shorter Catechism

Chapter 1:
Burdens & Rest

[28] "Come to me, all you who are weary and burdened, and I will give you rest. [29] Take my yoke upon you and learn from me, for I am gentle and humble in heart, and you will find rest for your souls. [30] For my yoke is easy and my burden is light." (Matthew 11:28-30)

When Jesus spoke these words to his disciples it was still early in his earthly ministry. Crowds of weary and burdened people were answering his call to "come to me" and find rest. Matthew in recording these verses did not specify the nature of the burdens or the source of the people's weariness, but judging from the context of the scripture and religious climate of Jesus' day, a good guess is that the burdens were the religious imperatives laid upon the people by the highly legalistic Pharisees, who insisted that faithful and observant Jews could only please God by following to the smallest detail the multitude of Hebrew laws. These laws covered every aspect of life: what you ate and didn't eat, when and where you worshiped, where you could and couldn't travel, what you touched and didn't touch, and the list goes on.

The Hebrew law in the hands of the Pharisees placed burdensomely high expectations on Jews trying to do the right thing, trying to please God. Then, Jesus comes on the scene, and using the very same scripture in which the Pharisees found the basis for imposing burdensome laws, Jesus tells the people that the "Lord of heaven and earth … has hidden things from the wise and learned, and revealed them to little children." (Matthew 11:25) After saying this, he issued his call to come to him, lay down your burden, and find rest. The Pharisees had gotten things wrong. Jesus' Father, who is the "Lord of heaven and earth" does "not delight in sacrifice" imposed by the Pharisees. Instead, what God requires is "a broken spirit; a broken and contrite heart" that reveals our trust and dependence upon Our Creator. (see Psalm 51:16-17) Jesus told the people they could learn to trust and depend upon God when they answered his call, and in knowing Jesus' "gentle and humble" heart that they would find "rest for [their] souls."

In our libertine, anything-goes Western lives, a society bound in a straitjacket of burdensome expectations of religious duties seems so strange and foreign. But, it shouldn't. If we honestly assess the way Western men and women live, we would see that our society places burdensomely high expectations on all of us – but especially the young – to succeed. If you want to be a success in life, then you need to follow the script, and the script of things we need to do is very lengthy. But, just like 1st Century Jews following the law, we work very hard to check every box on the road to success. Is it any wonder that we're burdened and weary?

The "wise and learned" in the West have loaded us up with what we must do in life, but what if, just like the Pharisees of Jesus' day, they're wrong? What if Jesus' call to come to him and find rest for our soul is just as needed and just as valid today as it was two thousand years ago? Where do we look to find rest for our souls? Jesus told us that this type of rest is "hidden … from the wise and learned, [but] revealed … to little children." Good children embody simplicity, innocence, and obedience, but there is another creature that exhibits these characteristics. Horses, and in the following story we'll find out what a horse can teach us.

* * *

From 1st Century Jerusalem to Baltimore, Maryland 1938

November 1, 1938 was a Tuesday. It was a work day, and an odd day to have such an important sporting event. But, this event had so captivated America that 40,000 people were in the stands and another 40 million, roughly a third of the population, listened on radio. It was the "Match of the Century." One-on-one, Seabiscuit, the race horse who had won the most prize money in 1937, was racing War Admiral that year's Triple Crown winner, who was considered the favorite. The horses were called to post, and took their place at the starting line on Baltimore's Pimlico Race Track. An excited announcer called the race:

They're head-and-head as they head for that home lane. Watch for them now as they turn into the stretch. Head-and-head. Both horses under a drive. This is a real horse race. Just what we'd hoped we'd get. They're head-and-head and both jockeys driving. It's the best horse from here in. They've got 200 yards to come. It's horse against horse. Both of them driving. Seabiscuit leads by a length. Now, Seabiscuit by a length and a half. Woolf has put away his whip. Seabiscuit by three! Seabiscuit by three! Seabiscuit is the winner by four lengths!

But, Seabiscuit's victory is the end of the story. Now, we must go back to the beginning.

"Hell, he's so beat up, it's hard to tell what he's like. I just can't help feelin' they got him so screwed up runnin' in a circle, he's forgotten what he was born to do. He just needs to learn how to be a horse again."

These lines are from the 2003 film, *Seabiscuit,* that was based on the best-selling book by Laura Hillenbrand. The book and movie tell the true story of the thoroughbred race horse, and this early assessment of Seabiscuit was given by horse trainer, Tom Smith, who was portrayed by actor, Chris Cooper. When

Smith first saw Seabiscuit, the horse was a basket case – unruly to the point of dangerous and losing races. Smith's diagnosis of the problem are the lines quoted above – "they got him so screwed up runnin' in a circle, he's forgotten what he was born to do." Great expectations were pinned to Seabiscuit in the beginning, but by the time Smith came on the scene just getting the horse out of his stall was a challenge. Millions of Americans, and more broadly Westerners in general, share Seabiscuit's anxiety – getting out of the front door and facing the world is a struggle! Like Seabiscuit, we're running in circles and have forgotten what we were born to do.

Seabiscuit was abused by the expectations that the horse racing industry placed on him. His bloodline was impeccable. He spent his formative years on the finest farms, receiving the best of care. He was trained in the ways of racing. The blinkers that covered his face, the feel of the bit in his mouth, the cinch of the saddle, the lightness of the jockey in the stirrups, and the sting of the whip were second nature to him. Expectations were high! This horse was going to win races and make lots of money! But then he didn't, and the problems begin to compound.

Veterinarians poked and prodded him. Trainers with their pet methods and latest techniques came and went. Jockeys coaxed and whipped him. Horse whispers talked to him, and the net result was an agitated and angry horse, who was worse off than when he entered the racing world. Despite their investment, Seabiscuit clearly wasn't living up to his owner's expectations. So, it is with Western men and women.

Parents invest in us. We're not just cared for, but pampered. We have the finest schooling. We're told we are special and have the potential to achieve anything to which we set our minds. We win awards. We earn degrees. We accumulate college debt with the anticipation of earning it all back and much more. Like Seabiscuit, the world's expectations for us are burdensomely high. But then, the great job doesn't materialize. Our pay is mediocre. Our college debt is like a weight around our necks. Our work is unfulfilling especially in light of our expectations. Relationships are superficial – where is that special someone just for me? In our despair, we search the Web for podcasts on coping strategies, we download books on how to achieve success and wealth. We commiserate with like-minded friends, and we conflate sex with love in our search for anything that might fill our souls. We carried the burden of great expectations into the world only to find ourselves walking in a circle and following bad advice. Truly, we are all Seabiscuits!

For Seabiscuit, the thoroughbred, the way out of his mess was to learn to be a horse again. Tom Smith, his trainer, took him far from the racing world. Gone were the barns, paddocks, tack rooms, grooms, and endless loops around oval tracks. Seabiscuit was released into a green pasture to graze with other horses. He was part of a herd. If it rained, he got wet. If he itched, he rolled in dirt. With the sun on his back and hindquarter to hindquarter with other horses, he chewed tender grass. His instinctual needs were filled. Seabiscuit was a horse again! Likewise, the way out of our mess is to learn how to be human again.

But, humans aren't horses. Horses are one of God's most beautiful creatures, but they are simple minded. Humans are just the opposite. We are not that much to look at, but we are highly intelligent and complex. Therefore, our first thought is that our need for meaning, purpose, and love cannot be satisfied through a simple act that corresponds to one messed up horse grazing with his herd. These needs, however, can be met through one simple act. Worship! When we worship, we are answering Jesus' call to:

"Come to me, all you who are weary and burdened, and I will give you rest. 29 Take my yoke upon you and learn from me, for I am gentle and humble in heart, and you will find rest for your souls. 30 For my yoke is easy and my burden is light."

Worship of Our Savior is humanity's green pasture. Our fellow worshipers – those sitting in the pews beside us or standing in the communion line with us – is our herd. Christ's sanctuary is our green pasture. Hymns, scripture, and sermons are the grasses upon which we graze. From their nourishment, we offer prayers and praise. Bound together by the holy cord of Christ's love, our herd navigates life with purpose. This is worship, and to understand how such a simple act satisfies our deepest human needs, we look again to Seabiscuit.

After a few months with the herd in the pasture, Tom Smith resumed Seabiscuit's race training. Smith's methods were similar to other trainers. Conditioning runs, sprints, time trials, practice loading in the starting gate, etc. – Smith did all the things that were the stock and trade of all horse trainers. What was different this time was Seabiscuit. The angry, dangerous, unpredictable horse was gone, and in his place was a horse with a new spirit. It was the calm, confident spirit of a winner. Something had transformed him.

The grass in the pasture wasn't magical. The other horses in the herd weren't special. The time spent with the herd wasn't long – a few months. What was different for Seabiscuit was the combination of three things. Remove any one of them, and Seabiscuit stays an unmanageable, skittish, and losing race horse. They are: the herd, rest, and trust. The herd reminded Seabiscuit what a horse is created to do, and it's not racing. Racing channels a horse's natural instincts into an endeavor that's artificial. Artificial doesn't mean that it's bad or wrong. It just means horses have to be trained to be transported in trailers, conditioned to respond to the jockey's commands, and accept a life on the move that is spent in a variety of stalls each with its on sounds and scents. But time with the herd – and returning to the herd periodically for refreshment – allowed Seabiscuit, even while in the grip his artificial world, never to forget that he is a horse and that there is a pasture and a herd waiting for him. Next is rest. Seabiscuit rested in the pasture, but recuperation of sore muscles and rehabilitation of aching joints do not explain his miraculous transformation. Only a spiritual rest explains the new spirit in him. Such rest comes from a body at peace, a mind that is clear, and an environment that is secure, which bring us to the most important ingredient in this transformation. Trust. Seabiscuit trusted Tom Smith. He trusted that his new trainer intended only good for him, and he responded to his commands.

Our pasture is Christ's sanctuary, and the three ingredients that changed Seabiscuit can change us. Our herd is our fellow worshipers. Together we remind one another that we humans are created for more than the artificial world in which we live. Like Seabiscuit, we are constantly on the move, and like the horse, we often work from stalls called cubicles. Yet in the midst of the rush of modern Western life, we know our herd is out there, and together we share the belief that we are eternal spiritual creatures, and that we are much more than a cog in the artificial world that we encounter daily. In no way does this imply that the artificial world of work, entertainment, sports, travel, and all the other things that make modern life fast paced and enjoyable are wrong or bad. It simply means that worshipping Jesus Christ with our herd reminds us of the deeper reality of who we are as a human being. Therefore, we gather weekly with our herd to worship Our Creator and be reminded of who we really are. Strengthened, we return on Monday to the artificial world, and like Seabiscuit, we are transformed by the time spent in God's pasture.

Rest is the second ingredient. Not enough time in the day and fatigue are common reoccurring complaints. Therefore, adding one more activity to an already jammed packed schedule is counterintuitive. Likewise, rest for an underperforming race horse, who was already losing money was counterintuitive. More training and more racing is surely the better prescription. But, it wasn't for Seabiscuit and it's not for us either. We need body, mind, and spiritual rest. Such a complete rest only comes from doing what we were born to do, and that is fellowship with God through daily prayer and weekly gathering for worship.

Daily private prayer is a necessity for obtaining spiritual rest. Westerners are quite receptive to learning about the restorative value of Eastern mediation techniques. Books, magazines, blogs, and podcasts that promise a healthier life, better sex, and clear, smoother skin due to mediation abound. We will even practice Feng shui, hoping that by raking a tiny tray of sand on our desk in certain patterns we will achieve inner peace. Eastern mediation does have certain value, but so did some of the unusual training techniques foisted on Seabiscuit. They, however, weren't natural to him. They weren't part of who he was, and neither is Eastern mediation for Westerners. Eastern mediation looks outward seeking to bring inside us a host of spirits, natural forces, or mantras to soothe our inward spirit and allow rest. Christian prayer looks upward seeking to bring inside us the living God, who transforms our inward spirit with his spirit, and in doing so shifts our focus from us to him, from ourselves to others, and from the now to the promise of eternity. This reordering is actually a restoring of what we were created to do, which is fellowship with God, and with this fellowship comes a natural spiritual rest. The Apostle Paul wrote in his Letter to the Romans, "Do not conform to the pattern of this world, but be transformed by the renewing of your mind." (Romans 12:2) The pattern of this world brings burdens and fatigue, while worship of Christ brings rest and renewal.

Worship, both in private prayer and a church service, is the acknowledgement and adoration of God, as Creator of all things, and acceptance of our position within his creation. We are not gods, and our relationship to God is not one of equals. When we bow our heads and hearts to God in worship, we are affirming this unequal relationship, and with this affirmation comes the rest of completeness. The Bible even gives this type of rest a special name calling it a "Sabbath rest."

9 *There remains, then, a Sabbath-rest for the people of God;* 10 *for anyone who enters God's rest also rests from their works just as God did from his.* 11 *Let us, therefore, make every effort to enter that rest...* (Hebrews 4:9-11)

Worship is where the human herd rests. Christ's sanctuary is the "green pastures" and "quiet waters" of Psalm 23. It is God who makes us "lie down in green pastures," and it is he, who leads us "beside quiet waters." In worship, we place ourselves in God's calm pasture, and "he refreshes" our souls. This is the Sabbath rest that restores us, and defines our humanity. Our time in God's secure pasture is where we learn how to be human. However, before we enter the pasture gate, we have to make a judgment. We have to decide on the third ingredient that transformed Seabiscuit. We have to decide whether or not to trust God.

Seabiscuit believed that Tom Smith intended only good for him. This was the starting point for his equine transformation. Likewise, it is the starting point for our human transformation. Do we believe that God only intends good for us? Do we trust God enough to enter his pasture, the church sanctuary, and experience the Sabbath rest? Or do we not trust him, and are content with the burdens and tiredness of life apart from Christ? One or the other must be chosen. There is no halfway in-between, and the starkness of this choice is written into Creation itself. It is the choice that Adam (every man) and Eve (every woman) made. The world's first couple believed a lie and thought they could "be like God" (Genesis 3:5), which is a burdensomely high expectation! It was an expectation they couldn't live into, and neither can we live into the West's great expectations. Like Adam and Eve, who became fugitives from God and hid among the trees of the garden even as their Creator searched for them calling, "Where are you?" (Genesis 3:8), so we hide from God too. Eden was gone for Adam and Eve, and there is not a Western Eden for us either. But, that's not the end of the story. Just as Seabiscuit's failure was not the end of his story but the beginning, so too is humankind's story.

The Bible tells us there is a new Eden prepared for us by Jesus Christ through his resurrection. (Revelation 22) When we worship, we are declaring our choice. We are placing our trust in God, and in doing so we experience the Sabbath rest of Christ's new Eden and we are transformed. Truly, we are all Seabiscuits! Through worship, we can enter God's pasture and be transformed. With the transformation, the burden of great expectations is lifted. No longer conforming to the West's expectations on how life should be lived, we now focus on how life ought to be lived, and that focus is on God, not ourselves.

This transformation does not happen overnight. It happens over a lifetime, and that's the difference between horses and humans. Seabiscuit's transformation happened over a period of months, because the purpose was to calm the horse and gain his trust so that he would be obedient to Smith's training techniques. The goal was to win races. Christ's goal for humans is not winning, but living, and the type of life that Christ wants for us is loving, gentle, humble, peaceful, restful, confident, and truthful. Day-by-day over a lifetime, Christ, whom we trust with our lives, trains these characteristics into us, because they are in him. When we are obedient to the commands of Our Trainer, the transformation begins.

This process takes time and we may not even perceive that it's happening. When we answer Jesus' call of "come to me… and… learn from me, for I am gentle and humble in heart, and you will find rest for your souls," our situation and the people around us do not magically change. Our college debt is not suddenly paid off, the boss who is really overbearing, critical, and watching our every move is still the same, our spouse, whose sloppiness we could once overlook, but now cannot abide, is still sloppy, our teenagers are still mouthy and disrespectful, and the list of difficult and challenging situations that we all face could go on and on. But, what's different is us, and how we feel about and react to the situations in which we live. The reason we're different is because Our Trainer is daily shaping our hearts by infusing his character into our character.

Jesus tells those who come to him to "take up their cross daily and follow me." (Luke 9:23) When people read this verse or hear a misinformed pastor preach on it, they all too often come away with self-absorbed ideas, imaging themselves to be some type of martyr carrying a cross, and their martyrdom can take on a multitude of forms. Perhaps, they imagine themselves doing missionary work in some foreign land under deplorable conditions. Or maybe their imagined martyrdom is closer to home, and their cross is that others cannot see what really good people they are. Unfortunately, these self-guided excursions take us away from Our Trainer's methods, and replaces what Christ wants for us with what we want or imagine for ourselves. Therefore, we need to look carefully at Christ's words. He calls us to him to learn from him "for I am gentle and humble in heart." Now, we are at the core of Our Trainer's method. To be transformed, our hearts must be gentle and humble like Christ's heart. And, from this starting point, the transformation begins.

How we think about, feel about, and react to our situations is much different. It's healthier and constructive.

That boss, who is overbearing? We are calmer now, our hearts are gentle and humble, and we are better able to think more clearly and address his dreadful management style. Now, you have the confidence to realize that perhaps the solution is to change jobs. Taking positive action – whatever it may be – is better than being angry and resentful all the time. The sloppy spouse and mouthy kids? Your new attitude toward them will over time influence how they treat you. You see transformation of our heart and character takes time, and it takes even more time to change our life situations, but this is what it means to "take up [your] cross daily and follow me." Whatever situation you're in, it means that you're sticking with Our Trainer, and making his ways your ways. It's not about winning. It's about living.

In this new life with Christ, we're never alone. When Seabiscuit was angry and unruly, he was so alone. Alone in his stall, because no one could go in. Alone in the racing industry, because no one wanted him. But, then Tom Smith found him, and now Seabiscuit had a pasture, a herd, and a trainer. Is it so different with us? Christ finds us, provides us not just a pasture, but a green pasture with quiet water, and he gives us not just rest, but a Sabbath rest. But, most importantly, he gives us himself and scripture to enable us to know him better, and we have a herd, fellow Christians, around us. With faith in him, he daily trains us, making his ways our ways, his heart our heart, and his desires our desires.

What can a horse teach us? That the West's burden of great expectations is just that, a burden. But, Jesus says, "Come to me, all you who are weary and burdened, and I will give you rest." No matter how difficult the race is before us, we always know that Jesus intends only good for us, and that God has prepared for us a green pasture beside quiet water. In God's pasture is where we learn how to be human again.

Chapter 2:
Truth and Righteousness

The Apostle John recorded in his gospel the dramatic events occurring the night that Jesus' was arrested. Pontius Pilate, the Roman governor, had Jesus flogged, and after the flogging, Roman soldiers pressed a crown of thorns onto Jesus' head and dressed him in a purple robe – the color reserved for royalty. When they were finished, they returned Jesus to Pilate, who then brought him out for all the people of Jerusalem to see. John captured the moment as follows:

4 Once more Pilate came out and said to the Jews gathered there, "Look, I am bringing him out to you to let you know that I find no basis for a charge against him." 5 When Jesus came out wearing the crown of thorns and the purple robe, Pilate said to them, "Here is the man!" (John 19: 4-5)

"Here is the man!" or "Behold the man!" in the King James Version appeared in the Latin Vulgate as *Ecce Homo*. Over the centuries, these two words inspired numerous artists to paint the scene of Jesus, battered and bleeding, standing next to Pilate on a balcony above an angry crowd. The drama and poignancy of the moment challenged the artistic ability of painters, who desired to capture the truth and meaning of the scene. Hieronymus Bosch (1475), Titian (1570), Caravaggio (1605), Cigoli (1607), and Ciseri (1871) are noteworthy painters of *Ecce Homo*.

Through their art, they desired to present truth, because the truth about sinful humanity and humanity's Savior are on full display in *Ecce Homo*. In fact, even Pilate at the time seemed to sense that truth was being revealed. Earlier in the night before Pilate had Jesus flogged and before he brought Jesus onto the balcony, John records this exchange between Jesus and the Roman governor.

[37] *"You are a king, then!" said Pilate.*

Jesus answered, "You say that I am a king. In fact, the reason I was born and came into the world is to testify to the truth. Everyone on the side of truth listens to me."

[38] *"What is truth?" retorted Pilate.* (John 18:37-38)

Pilate's question rings through the ages. What is truth? A companion question also confronts Western men and women today: where is truth? We live in the Information Age yet where do we find truth? Is truth found in churches? Sometimes yes, and sometimes no. Churches sadly stray from God's truth. Perhaps, truth is found in Western law, justice, and in our universities and institutions? But, we know from experience that truth is not there. A better question is: where did previous generations find truth? The *Ecce Homo* paintings provide a clue. The artists cited above span 400 years, and while lengthy, this time period is but a subset of the thousands of years where scripture was the source of truth. The artists' task was to capture truth on canvass. In *Ecce Homo* the truth of Christ, the power of Rome, and the anger of the mob in divine conflict are represented in their art. Where do today's artists look for truth, and what does their choice of subject matter tell us about what truth is and where it is found? Let's meet an artist, who will tell us.

* * *

From 1st Century Jerusalem to London, 2014

"Art is an attempt to get to the very center of truth. It never can, but it can get quite close." These are the words of Anselm Kiefer, a German born painter, sculptor, and writer on the opening of his exhibition at the Royal Academy in London in 2014.[1] What is the center of truth, the reality of our world, that Kiefer sees? Before discerning truth as presented in Kiefer's art, it is necessary to know his personal story, because it shapes the art he creates. His story and his art tells how the West sees itself and understands truth in the 21st Century.

Anselm Kiefer, the son of an art teacher, was born in southwestern Germany on March 8, 1945. The date is important, because it was two months before Germany's surrender that ended the European theater of World War II. Kiefer was born into the rubble and devastation that was post-war Germany. His childhood was spent navigating the tangible, physical destruction of homes, roads, schools, and factories to name a few, but there was intangible destruction too that weighed on the German people. It was guilt – guilt over two wars and the Holocaust. What had this highly educated, industrialized, and Christian nation wrought upon the world? These tangible and intangible burdens were set within the context of the Cold War, where yet another great war loomed on the horizon, and Germany was ground zero. The German state was partitioned into two nations. The Soviet Union controlled and enslaved East Germany in communist ideology, and the United States and her allies were in charge of West Germany that was a free capitalist nation.

Kiefer's childhood is like a crucible for modern Western civilization. Crucibles are heat resistant ceramic containers that hold mixtures of metals and chemicals, which are then fired in an open flame. Once cooled, what is left inside is an amorphous mass that must be picked through to find what is desirable and useful, and separate it from worthless dross. Kiefer's formative years – and by extension the formative mid-20th Century years for all Westerners – was lived in the cooling amorphous mass of post-war Western civilization. For a coherent civilization to emerge, the hard work to find what was desirable, useful, and most importantly truthful, because truth had seemingly failed the West, had to be done. Instead of doing the hard work of examining the West's foundational religion that is Judeo-Christianity to determine if the religion had failed because it was untrue or if men had failed the religion because they believed lies, generations of Western intellectuals, artists, scientists, and writers adopted a pseudo-intellectual rejection of Judeo-Christianity. Theirs was not a search for truth, but a wholesale judgment, declaring that only worthless dross could emerge from Christian nations fired in the crucible of war. The religion, philosophy, science, institutions, governments, and nations so willingly yoked to wage war, surely, when melted down by war, could afford nothing of lasting merit for building a new world. Therefore, the work of the gifted, talented, and intellectual class was directed toward describing and critiquing the dross they saw.

With seemingly scarcely a thought, they said that Judeo-Christianity was part of the problem, and that the civilization built on the religion, morals, ethics, and scripture of the faith were unsuitable for a modern post-war West. Rather than seeking an enduring teleological truth buried in the West's amorphous mass, Kiefer appears to have opted to present a critical descriptive truth that tells who we are, and what Western civilization is like today. The truth that Kiefer apparently sees is filtered through the lens given him by the West's intellectual elites. The elitist lens filters out the past, blocks the future, and allows only analytical self-loathing through to the artist's eye. Therefore, what appears in selections of Kiefer's art is a brooding dusk of a civilization that has been judged. Not surprisingly, the center of the truth represented in his art is stationary. Like a portrait painter studying the lines, shadows, and texture of his subject's face, Kiefer's gaze seemingly never leaves the amorphous mass. His art tells us what our post-war melted civilization looks like, and he is good at it, which is why his art is celebrated and exhibited by major galleries and museums.

The 2014 Royal Academy exhibition featured several of Kiefer's watercolors and sculptures. A piece made specially for the Academy exhibition is entitled "Ages of the World." It is a large and imposing stack of rubble that fills an entire gallery. The stack is composed of old art canvasses placed flat one on top of the other, and interspersed among the canvasses are bits and pieces of debris. Metal rods randomly protrude from the stack like octopus tentacles that are searching, flailing, and hoping to touch something living, but only finding the dead. The Royal Academy catalogue described "Ages of the World," as part totem and part funeral pyre, and art writer, Alex Danchev said, "One might add part pyramid, part tomb; part sacrifice, part pile of the artist's signature stuff. Awed visitors circle it, a little warily. The material is infused with meaning; the stuff tells stories." Danchev continued writing, "There is a place for belief in the Kiefer worldview, belief in something above and beyond the featherless biped, but not a "salvator" or saviour. The artist's outlook is perhaps more intellectual than spiritual."[2]

Kiefer's watercolors were also exhibited in the Royal Academy. As a sculptor and painter, Kiefer shares a place in the artistic community with Rodin, who likewise was a sculptor and painter in watercolors. And, they share another bond: war. Rodin died near Paris in November 1917, a year before World War I ended, and Kiefer was born at the end of World War II. Both witnessed firsthand the destruction of civilization by war. Therefore, it's not surprising that in 2013, the Musée Rodin invited Kiefer to offer a 21st Century interpretation of the famous sculptor's 1914 book, *The Cathedrals of France*. For this hundredth anniversary, Kiefer created a whole new body of work for the update, and one painting, a watercolor, bears the name of book.[3]

Kiefer's watercolor, "The Cathedrals of France," is provocative. An impressionist rendering of the front façade of a Gothic cathedral fills the canvass. In the center is the cathedral's rose window, and Kiefer captures the hues typical of stained-glass windows, particularly blue. What stands out in the rose window, however, are not the colors, but the panels that come together to form a nude female seductively lying prostrate. According to Kiefer the work was inspired by Rodin's comparison of the structure of cathedrals to the female body. Kiefer agreed with Rodin that cathedrals should not be restored, but left to age and decay. Kiefer said, "For me, the process of getting old, of falling down – that is the *Cathédrals de France*."[4] One message of the painting is: the old ways of religion are gone; they were seductive in their time; now let them fall down. Kiefer's art has been summarized as follows: "The Kiefer world is a free world, but a heavily burdened one, full of dead souls. Kiefer's art is, among other things, an inquest and a reckoning – a reckoning with the history of the terrible 20th Century."[5]

The acclaim that Kiefer's art receives is because it does, as he said, present the center of truth about the West, as it is understood by the gifted, intellectual class that in turn drives culture. We are a free people, but heavily burdened in their eyes, and the question is: how did this happen? Surely, war is not wholly responsible, because wars always have antecedents, movements, causes, and thinking that inch civilizations into war. In the book, <u>Modern Times, The World From the Twenties to the Nineties</u>, noted British historian and author, Paul Johnson, provides an answer. The passage below summarizes how 19th Century ideas were the beginning of a moral and spiritual dusk that turned to darkness in the 20th Century.

Marx described a world in which the central dynamic was economic interest. To Freud, the principal thrust was sexual. Both assumed that religion, the old impulse which moved men and masses, was fantasy and always had been. Friedrich Nietzsche, the third of the trio, was also an atheist. But he saw God not as an invention but as a casualty, and his demise as in some important sense an historical event which would have dramatic consequences. He wrote in 1886: "The greatest event of recent time – that 'God is Dead,' that the belief in the Christian God is no longer tenable – is beginning to cast its first shadows over Europe." Among the advanced races, the decline and ultimately the collapse of the religious impulse would leave a huge vacuum. The history of modern times is in great part the history of how that vacuum had been filled. Nietzsche rightly perceived that the most likely candidate would be what he called the "Will to Power."[6]

Johnson's historical analysis offers a snapshot of a pre-war West that was giddy with ideas, and Kiefer's art captures the terrible burdensome aftermath of those ideas. It is a melted civilization "full of dead souls." In the 19th Century, the West's ongoing rejection of Judeo-Christianity accelerated, and to use Johnson's words, " the decline and ultimately the collapse of the religious impulse would leave a huge vacuum," leaving only the "Will to Power" and the exercise of it in war. In the late 20th and early 21st Centuries, the rejection of the faith, church, and scripture continues. The question for Western men and women today is: where do we go from here?

Where is the truth in Western art, literature, religion, philosophy, politics, and institutions that says, "Here is truth! Come to it! Embrace it! It will lead you!"? We are stagnant, stationary, we stare at the amorphous mass that is our civilization trying to capture every detail of the mess while offering nothing to build on, nothing to aspire to, and nothing to hope for. This is what passes for brilliance in today's West! Meanwhile, churches sit largely empty and, if thought of at all, many Westerners – perhaps most – would think Kiefer's nude projected on the front of a cathedral would be funny and artistically clever! Such is our haughty, smug, unrighteous dismissiveness that does nothing to answer: where do we go from here? Rod Dreher in The Benedict Option, A Strategy for Christians in a Post-Christian Nation argues it's time for Christians to opt-out of society to form, as much as possible, their own insular communities. Drawing upon the centuries-old monastic movement, Dreher advocates for a modern adoption of the Benedictine monastery. [7]

Benedict of Nursia was born in the late 5th Century, and was educated in Rome. For three years, he practiced an extreme form of asceticism, and lived in a cave south of Rome. A nearby monastery took him in and appointed him as their abbot. His strict discipline sparked rebellion among the monks, who attempted to poison him. Recognizing his need to change, Benedict created the Rule in 529 CE to govern monastic life. The Rule balanced ascetism with freedom, while providing a workable governing structure. From the Rule came the Benedictine Order, where, according to church historian, Bruce Shelley, "the monastic life [was] a kind of garrison for Christ in a hostile world." [8] Dreher's thinking is that the West is now so hostile to Christianity that it is time for Christian families to come together in a new garrison to preserve the faith, educate their children, and protect themselves from a society that disregards truth and celebrates sin.

The Benedict Option has sparked vigorous debate in Christian circles. Is it possible to actually separate and insulate oneself and family in today's connected world? If it is possible, is it desirable? After all, Christ lived in a pagan, sinful world that was hostile to Jews and his ministry in particular, and he certainly did not separate from society, but engaged it at all levels. This debate, however, obscures the real crisis. While Christian's debate whether or not it's best to practice truth and righteousness apart from or in society, the West slips deeper into depravity. Generations continue to be taught there is no God and no truth, and that righteousness is simply the hate-filled judgmental name for the way Christians choose to live. There is only one way to alleviate this crisis. We must renew our minds. The Apostle Paul in his letter to the church in 1st Century Rome wrote:

> *Do not conform to the pattern of this world, but be transformed by the renewing of your mind. Then you will be able to test and approve what God's will is—his good, pleasing and perfect will.* (Romans 12:2)

The pattern of today's Western world can be summed up in a single word: tiredness. We are tired of the smug and hollow intellectualism that masquerades as truth. We are tired of being lectured to by an elitist class, whose basis of morality comes from the editorial pages of the New York Times and what's trending on Twitter. We are tired of watching the faith that shaped the goodness our lives and undergirds the freedom and prosperity of Western Civilization being mocked and ridiculed by cheap pretenders, who are merely godless bullies. When we summons the courage to reject the tired old pattern of this world, our minds are freed and the renewal can begin. With this act of courage and faith, we realize that we are not alone. Christ, the source of truth, is with us, and to find truth, we go to the same source that inspired the painters of *Ecce Homo*. We go to scripture.

Let's return to Pilate's question. What is truth? Curiously, the Gospel of John contains no record of Jesus answering the governor's question. We can only speculate as to why, but perhaps, John did not record an answer, because the question had already been answered. The Gospel of John begins with Creation, and the apostle writes the following about Jesus:

9 The true light that gives light to everyone was coming into the world. 10 He was in the world, and though the world was made through him, the world did not recognize him. 11 He came to that which was his own, but his own did not receive him. 12 Yet to all who did receive him, to those who believed in his name, he gave the right to become children of God— 13 children born not of natural descent, nor of human decision or a husband's will, but born of God. (John 1:9-13)

These verses summarize the central truth of Christianity that is: through faith in Christ, we are saved, and have "the right to become children of God." That "those who believe in his name" are "born of God" is a bold claim to truth, but underlying this claim is one even more bold, which is this: at the center of all life and all creation is goodness and a God, who loves us. Evil, while it seems so strong and prevalent, is not at the center of life. God intends good for us. That's why Jesus came into the world, and he explained that to Pilate saying, "In fact, the reason I was born and came into the world is to testify to the truth. Everyone on the side of truth listens to me." This statement prompted Pilate's question, "What is truth?"

Truth is the word of God as written in scripture. It's not scientific truth, where things are measured, weighed, and put into a mathematical formula. It is a deeper truth revealed to humankind by God over thousands of years and preserved in scripture. Just as Western men and women are tired of smug intellectualism that masquerades as truth, aren't we equally – if not more – tired of the false choice that the West forces upon us? The choice is this: do you believe in science or the Bible? How utterly stupid! Science it not a belief. It is merely a reproducible explanation of Nature. Nature, however, is the physical realm set within a much deeper spiritual context. To know this spiritual context is to know the truth of God, and this truth is found in scripture. From God's truth comes righteousness, i.e., right living, and it is generations of right-living people who built our civilization. This is our inheritance.

As heirs, we too can know truth and live righteous lives, and the starting point for changing our lives is scripture. If you don't have one, buy a study Bible, and be sure to read the footnotes too. Find Bible commentaries and Christian books to help you. That's where you'll discover truth and learn about righteousness. Pray and worship. These things can and should be done daily, which now brings us to the church and Sabbath worship.

Christian worship is fellowship with God and like-minded believers. Worship is the deepest expression of who we really are. Worship is where we creatures, who are created in the image of God, are home. When churches teach truth and righteousness, fellowship always follows and churches flourish. But sadly, finding a flourishing church is difficult. Please don't despair. First and foremost, as a Christian, you are a member of Christ's spiritual kingdom. Churches, whether ancient cathedrals or simple country churches, are physical outposts of Christ's spiritual kingdom. If you can find a physical outpost, where Christ's spirit is very present, count it as a great blessing. If, however, your church experience is uncomfortable boredom and spiritual deadness, pray that God will bring you to a better church and also that God will awaken all Western churches. On the day that God awakens the church, will be the day that truth and righteousness return to Western civilization. May our prayers hasten that day!

Amen

10/10/22

Chapter 3:
Repentance and Redemption

[14] Then Peter stood up with the Eleven, raised his voice and addressed the crowd: "Fellow Jews and all of you who live in Jerusalem, let me explain this to you; listen carefully to what I say.

" 'In the last days, God says,
I will pour out my Spirit on all people.
Your sons and daughters will prophesy,
your young men will see visions,
your old men will dream dreams." (Acts 2:14, 17)

With these words, Peter announced that the Spirit of God, aka the Holy Spirit, had just come into the world in a new, dramatic, and very personal way. Christians refer to this event as Pentecost, because it occurred fifty days after Christ's resurrection and in the Greek New Testament, Pentecost literally translates as "fifty celebrate." Pentecost happened in Jerusalem, and before his ascension, Jesus instructed his disciples to stay in Jerusalem and wait. Luke recorded the specific instructions in Acts 1.

"Do not leave Jerusalem, but wait for the gift my Father promised, which you have heard me speak about. [5] For John baptized with water, but in a few days you will be baptized with the Holy Spirit." (Acts 1:4-5)

Jerusalem wasn't the safest place for the disciples to stay. After all, their leader had just been crucified, and now they were supposed to remain in Jerusalem and wait an indeterminate length of time for an unspecified gift. That took faith! Days later their faith was rewarded with the coming of the Holy Spirit that Luke described as follows:

Suddenly a sound like the blowing of a violent wind came from heaven and filled the whole house where they were sitting. [3] *They saw what seemed to be tongues of fire that separated and came to rest on each of them.* [4] *All of them were filled with the Holy Spirit and began to speak in other tongues as the Spirit enabled them.* (Acts 2:1-4)

People on the Jerusalem streets heard the commotion coming from the house, and when the disciples emerged, they confronted a bewildered crowd. The crowd was further confused when the disciples, several who were simple fishermen, began to fluently speak foreign languages that were understandable to the various nationalities in Jerusalem for Passover and a subsequent festival. Language students plodding along would love to produce such fluency so quickly!

After Peter calmed the crowd, he began explaining what was happening by citing prophesy and quoting King David. This context was important so that the people could grasp the significance of Christ's crucifixion, resurrection, and their complicity in the crucifixion. Here is the concluding line from Peter's Pentecost sermon along with the people's response and the action they must take.

[36] *"Therefore let all Israel be assured of this: God has made this Jesus, whom you crucified, both Lord and Messiah."*

[37] *When the people heard this, they were cut to the heart and said to Peter and the other apostles, "Brothers, what shall we do?"*

[38] *Peter replied, "Repent and be baptized, every one of you, in the name of Jesus Christ for the forgiveness of your sins. And you will receive the gift of the Holy Spirit.* [39] *The promise is for you and your children and for all who are far off—for all whom the Lord our God will call."* (Acts 2:36-39)

The sound of violent wind from the house, the crowd, multiple languages spoken fluently, and Peter's sermon all happened on the streets of Jerusalem. It was a public event, and likewise, their repentance was public. The scriptures say that when the people understood their part in Jesus' crucifixion "they were cut to the heart" and seeing their repentance, Peter told them that Jesus Christ offers forgiveness and redemption. Now, they should be baptized to receive the Holy Spirit and live a new and different type of life; a life in fellowship with God, and that fellowship is expressed through worship.

Peter's sermon and the subsequent repentance, redemption, and baptisms (about 3,000 were baptized) began with a prophesy from the second chapter of Joel.

"'In the last days, God says,
I will pour out my Spirit on all people.
Your sons and daughters will prophesy,
your young men will see visions,
your old men will dream dreams." (Joel 2:28)

From Pentecost until today, God has not withdrawn his Spirit, but Western men and women have withdrawn from God. As a result, our sons and daughters no longer know the words of God for that is what prophesy is, our young men can no longer see visions of heaven and therefore cannot envision an earthly society that is moral and just, and our old men can no longer dream dreams of the heart of God touching the heart of all people. Westerners are focused on the here and now, and what's in it for me. Repentance for such people is truly a difficult proposition, because unlike the people in Jerusalem on the day of Pentecost, Westerners being "cut to the heart" by the gravity of our sins and repenting seems impossible. But, sadly the opposite – celebrating our sins – is a common everyday occurrence. Yet even as we celebrate sin, we cannot escape the West's Judeo-Christian foundational story, and central to our story is the repentance and redemption of Pentecost. Therefore,

Western societies on occasion expect at least a show of repentance even from the famous and powerful.

In capitalist societies, demand creates products and services, and a new service industry has developed in the past two decades. It is the apology industry. This industry is to repentance and redemption what artificial sweeteners are to sugar. These man-made substitutes are sweet, but they are not real sugar, nor do they have any calories, i.e., they do nothing to change the body. Likewise, the apology industry appears to have the humility of repentance, but it's not real and it does nothing, i.e., requires no change in the so-called repentant person. Fake apologies and faux repentance have significant societal consequences. They are hardened hearts, a been-there-done-that jaundiced view of the world, and a character that delights in craftiness, as in look what I got away with! These are characteristics of a people, who have no expectation of authenticity and no hope of genuineness from themselves or others. Can such a people be "cut to the heart"? Can Westerners truly repent and receive Christ's redemption? Let's see.

* * *

From 1st Century Jerusalem to Washington, DC 1998

"As anyone close to me knows, for months I have been grappling with how best to reconcile myself to the American people, to acknowledge my own wrongdoing and still to maintain my focus on the work of the presidency." This was the opening statement in President Bill Clinton's public apology to the nation for his sexual affair with the young White House intern, Monica Lewinsky. The date of the apology was December 11, 1998, and the president was facing impeachment in the House of Representatives and removal from office, if convicted by the Senate.

Impeachment was the culmination of a year-long series of hearings, investigations, denials, and politics Washington-style. Nineteen ninety-eight begin with the president issuing a strong denial of any wrong doing. At the conclusion of a January 26 White House speech, Clinton said, "I want to say one thing to the America people. I want you listen to me. I'm going to say this again. I did not have sexual relations with that woman, Miss Lewinsky. I never told anybody to lie not a single time. Never! These allegations are false, and I need to go back to work for the American people. Thank you." By the end of the year, President Clinton was boxed-in and forced to admit that he had lied. He did have an affair with Monica Lewinsky, and the December speech was his public apology. wow

Students of history can judge for themselves whether or not President Clinton was "cut to the heart" and truly repentant. What is undeniable is that he was caught and fighting to stay in power. Central to that effort was the December speech, and it was a masterpiece of public relations craftsmanship. Monica Lewinsky was never mentioned, and the president never repented for preying upon a star-struck young woman. She more than anyone else bore the brunt of their affair, and yet where was the shame, confession, and repentance for what he had done to her? That's the craftsmanship of this speech. Generic wrongdoing was acknowledged, but the specific wrong and the victim were veiled in high-minded platitudes. The platitudes that Clinton's speechwriters chose were Ben Franklin, who was quoted, and an unidentified poet, who penned a few verses about moving on. How convenient! Clinton ended the speech by looking to the future and all the important work that he needed to accomplish. He said, "That is simply all I can do – the work of the American people."

It was a brilliant speech. It's a tough call. So much has happened so quickly, but that December 1998 speech may have been the birth of the apology industry. Today, well-crafted public apologies are not rare. Hollywood stars, professional athletes, sports broadcasters, media personalities, senators, congressmen, members of Western parliaments, CEO's of the world's largest corporations, presidents and prime ministers, members of royal families, and even overly self-important bloggers and internet influencers offer apologies with a promise to do better. Invariably they say they are much better people now and therefore, much better positioned to do the important work that lies ahead. And, it doesn't really matter what that work actually is. Apologies with faux repentance, i.e., vowing to change when there is really no intention to do so, are so ubiquitous that PR firms offer services on how to send the perfect message and strike just the right tone.

How to offer just the right apology, exhibit an appropriate amount of contrition, and promise – without promising too much – to do better is the subject of articles in business school journals. The Harvard Business Review in a 2015 article entitled, "The Organizational Apology" presented a roadmap for the perfect apology including when to make it, because there are dangers in making it too early or too late. The authors, who are faculty at the world's top business schools of Harvard, Wharton, and Columbia, even delved into the psychology of why it's so hard to make apologies and so easy to get them wrong. They wrote, "Let's recognize two facts about apologies at the outset: First, we are psychologically predisposed to find reasons (or excuses) to delay or avoid saying we're sorry. Apologizing feels uncomfortable and risky. There's a loss of power or face involved—it rearranges the status hierarchy and makes us beholden, at least temporarily, to the other party. That doesn't feel good. So, it's no wonder people try to avoid dwelling on or drawing attention to mistakes and that when one is pointed out, they get defensive, arguing their side of the story and shifting blame to others."[9]

The professors' observation that an apology "rearranges the status hierarchy and makes us beholden" identifies the actual purpose of an apology, and more importantly repentance. The professors' guidance in the Harvard Business Review article, and the reason people pay big bucks to PR firms, is so that the loss of power and rearrangement of "the status hierarchy" is as painless and temporary as possible. Apologies are so readily made and repentance is offered so effortlessly today because they are meaningless and cheap. You're caught! Now, get out in front of the wrong-doing, screw-up, problem, or whatever is the unpleasant issue and get it over with. Be contrite, promise change, minimize culpability, and move on. Even better, if you can attribute your wrong-doing to long held, but mistaken and misguided social norms that you now know are wrong, i.e., you're "woke," then you can turn the tables. You don't lose face or power, but actually gain status, because you are seen as newly virtuous; hence, the term virtue-signaling.

The West's cheap, hollow, ubiquitous, high-sounding, virtue-signaling apology mania has crushed authenticity out of the Western character. An authentic person is truthful to themselves and God. Such a truthful person – to borrow from a line from Hamlet – "canst not then be false to any man." An authentic person is someone who can be "cut to the heart," because they see the pain they've caused others. As a consequence, they experience emotions that are exceedingly rare in the West – guilt and shame. A person, who sees the pain of others is "cut to the heart," repents, asks for mercy, and seeks redemption. But today in the West, the apology industry has so perfected faux repentance that no matter how disgusting the behavior or the damage to someone like Monica Lewinsky, guilt and shame are never experienced or exhibited. The weird thing is that we all know it's phony, which raises important questions. What does the willingness of Western men and women to accept faux repentance say about us? Let's be clear: it's not that we truly accept phony apologies, because our so-called acceptance and forgiveness is phony too! It's all a con, and we participate in it so what does this say about the moral and spiritual character of our souls? Is it possible for us to experience the guilt and shame that produces true repentance?

The soul and character of a people so willingly manipulated by obvious phoniness is a society where nothing is sacred, not even human life, and certainly nothing is holy, not God, not the church, not communion, not baptism, not marriage, not love, not virtue, not honor – nothing. When nothing is sacred and nothing is holy, the pain that you have caused to others and equally important, to God is likewise nothing to you. Therefore, nothing cuts you to the heart. The soul of such people is a wasteland that is barren of truth and filled with lies. Our souls are so easily filled with fakery, because far too many Westerners believe there is no God, there is no truth, there is no right and wrong, there is no judgment, and therefore, there is no need for us to repent and receive redemption. Souls where the truth of God has been exchanged for the lies of modernity are easily manipulated. The faux repentance of the apology industry is such child's play it's a wonder that PR firms get paid so much money. Because you see, we are willing participants in their fraud. And, we participate in the fraud, because we cannot believe that the soul and character of a person, including ourselves, can be genuine. Is it possible for us to be "cut to the heart," repent, and be baptized like the people of Jerusalem on that day of Pentecost? Yes, it is, but we need to be truthful to ourselves and God, i.e., we need to be authentic.

An authentic person places a single virtue at the center of their character. That virtue is humility. Andrew Murray (1828-

1917), a South African pastor and writer, described the importance of humility as follows:

> *Humility, the place of entire dependence on God, is, from the very nature of things the first duty and the highest virtue of the creature, and the root of every virtue. And so pride, or the loss of humility, is the root of every sin and evil.*[10]

This juxtaposition of humility and pride takes us to Creation, Eden, and the choice that Adam and Eve made, which was the humility of being dependent upon God versus the pride of declaring ourselves gods. It is not a one-time choice. A humble heart versus a prideful heart are two different shapes of a life lived. A seed planted where it has access to all the things that Creation deemed necessary for it to thrive grows into a beautiful tree, and likewise, the opposite happens too. A seed cutoff from the things of Creation is stunted, gnarled, and ugly. So, it is too with the shape of our lives. A humble heart grows into a life of goodness and beauty that is authentic to what God intended life to be. A prideful heart grows into a withered life of bitterness that is inauthentic and discredits what God intended life to be. In this juxtaposition of two very different kind of lives, we see the power of Christ's resurrection. Repentance, forgiveness, and redemption are possible. God can change the shape of our hearts and lives, but we need to be truthful about who we are, including the sins we have committed. The phoniness of the apology industry gets us nowhere with God. We must be truthful to ourselves and God.

To be truthful to ourselves and God, we must look into our souls and see, not what we want the world to see about ourselves, but what God sees. The Lord God of scripture is the source and light of truth, but we need a mirror to reflect God's truth into our souls, and God has provided one. Christ is that mirror. The writer of Hebrews tells us that Christ, "the Son is the radiance of God's glory and the exact representation of his being." (Hebrews 1:3) Being fully human, Jesus empathizes with us and reflects God's glory and truth into our souls, and when God's truth shines in our souls, we are "cut to the heart" and can repent. Therefore, with a prayerful heart, let's begin shining the light of God's scripture into our soul, and the passage we select is Psalm 102.

This psalm is entitled as "a prayer of an afflicted person who has grown weak and pours out a lament before the Lord." The early Christian church used this psalm as a penitential prayer yet the psalm contains no confession of specific sins. Perhaps, the 1st and 2nd Century church recognized that before specific sins can be confessed, we must confess the generic sinful condition of our hearts, i.e., we must be truthful about who we really are. We must be authentic. Although written thousands of years ago, Psalm 102 peers deep into the 21st Century Western soul, and speaks truth.

Psalm 102

Hear my prayer, Lord;
let my cry for help come to you.
2 *Do not hide your face from me*
when I am in distress.
Turn your ear to me;
when I call, answer me quickly.
3 *For my days vanish like smoke;*
my bones burn like glowing embers.
4 *My heart is blighted and withered like grass;*
I forget to eat my food.
5 *In my distress I groan aloud*
and am reduced to skin and bones.
6 *I am like a desert owl,*
like an owl among the ruins.
7 *I lie awake; I have become*
like a bird alone on a roof.

Like wiping a steamy fog from a bathroom mirror, the psalmist allows us to see our own reflection. The mist covering the mirror is the distorted way we perceive and present ourselves, which is strong, assertive, and demanding a better world. Westerners insist on a world of social justice and equity without limits, including gender fluidity. Nothing is off limits if it helps achieve our vision. Vulgar language, lawsuits, outing, lecturing, doxing, hectoring, and indulging whether it's sex, alcohol, or something else – these and more are constituents of the swirling fog of Western life that the psalmist wipes away to reveal the true suffering hearts of sinful Western men and women. The psalmist's words truthfully express the barrenness of the Western soul.

Verses 6 and 7 tell of the quiet desperation locked away in the hearts of Westerners, particularly young women. These verses are worth reading again:

6 I am like a desert owl,
like an owl among the ruins.
7 I lie awake; I have become
like a bird alone on a roof.

Westerners are at once both the huntress desert owl and the lonely bird. To the Israelite psalmist, owls were unclean animals. (Deuteronomy 14:14-17) When "desert" is added as a descriptor, the scriptures are referring to ruined civilizations such as ancient Babylon. In the psalmist's mind's eye, this unclean bird relentlessly soars back and forth in the night sky, hunting prey. It swoops in and out of crumbling half-standing, half-collapsed structures that once were grand buildings. The predator lands and perches on a wobbly stone column, searching the moonlit shadows for any movement, any sign of life that it may devour. Finding none, this bird of prey will settle for carrion.

Countless numbers of Western men and women are desert owls. They see themselves as powerful birds of prey, swift and cunning, and ready to strike with sharp talons. They will gladly tear into anyone who stands in their way or moves against them for that is what they are trained to do. Their power comes from the night, from the cover of darkness. In their darkness, they hunt on social media, in bars and restaurants, at work, in organizations aimed at saving the planet, defeating world hunger, or promoting transgender rights. They hunt at play, whether it's biking, hiking, photography, or hot yoga, and they hunt at concerts, plays, sporting events, and of course parties. The objects of their hunt are things of the heart: meaning, love, acceptance, purpose, hope, forgiveness, redemption, and a home. The truly saddest part of the lives of Western desert owls is that they hunt in dry barren spiritual ruins and don't even know it.

The West's great spiritual structures – Eden's flash of light at Creation; Noah's faith to build an ark to save a sinful world; Abraham's faith that God would give him a son, Isaac; Joseph's faith that God would not abandon him as a slave in Egypt; Moses faith in confronting Pharaoh and leading slaves to freedom; David's faith, confidence, and hope in the Lord God that is expressed in the 23rd Psalm; the faith of Mary and Joseph in the stable with baby Jesus; the power of Jesus over death when he called Lazarus out of the grave; Jesus' command over all nature when he calmed the storm; the humility and love of Jesus as he washed his disciples' feet; the suffering of Jesus on the cross and the hope of his empty tomb, Peter's understanding that Christ's salvation is for all people when he baptized the Roman centurion, Cornelius and his family; the presence of the Holy Spirit with Paul in prison, allowing him to write of love and hope even while he suffered in a Roman dungeon – all these and more were the moral, spiritual, intellectual, and philosophical wood, stone, and mortar that built Western civilization, and today mostly lie in ruins, the hunting ground of desert owls, who cannot image the once great spiritual abundance of the wasteland they now prowl. Because very few real, genuine, living things exist in Western spiritual ruins, our desert owls eat carrion, mistaking sex for love, a career for meaning, likes on social media for acceptance, a cause for purpose, a new puppy for friendship, and a house with WIFI for a home. Despite the sharpness of her talons and the strength of her wings, the Western desert owl gains no spiritual sustenance from her prey, and her hunger is a loneliness of the soul. And, this loneliness awakens a different type of bird that cohabits the Western soul.

Like the psalmist, countless numbers of Western men and women "lie awake, and have become like a bird alone on a roof." In these ancient verses, the psalmist has captured the poignant duality of the Western heart. The huntress owl and a lonely bird live in the same heart. As the psalmist pictured the desert owl among the ruins, likewise, he pictured a lonely bird at dusk. She is perched atop a roof. It is winter. It will soon be dark and cold. Where is her nest? Where is her flock? Where is her home? Today, Western men and women lie awake. They feel the coming cold. The darkness is around them. They will not hunt tonight. The powerful desert owl has given way to the lonely bird. Alone, they have no one to comfort them and no shelter from the cold darkness.

The psalmist even tells us why so many Westerners are in such a dismal predicament. In verses 9 through 11, he writes:

For I eat ashes as my food
and mingle my drink with tears
10 *because of your great wrath,*
for you have taken me up and thrown me aside.

[11] My days are like the evening shadow;
I wither away like grass.

The Lord God has "great wrath" against the West, and he had "taken [us] up and thrown [us] aside," allowing the West to become a spiritual desert, because we will not, to use the business professors' words, "rearrange the status hierarchy" that repentance requires. We are in control, not God – if there is even a God! We will certainly not surrender any power to God or be beholden to him. The question is: how much longer will we allow the desert owl and lonely bird residence in our hearts? There is only one way to evict them. Repent. Cut them from our hearts, with the same knife that cut the hearts of the people of Jerusalem, when they recognized that in their sin, they had crucified Christ. God stands ready, urging us to repent. The psalmist of so long ago tells us, that God will "arise and have compassion" on us. He writes:

But you, Lord, sit enthroned forever;
your renown endures through all generations.
[13] You will arise and have compassion on Zion,
for it is time to show favor to her;
the appointed time has come. (Psalm 102:12-13)

When the West's appointed time has come, and this generation repents, and is "baptized, every one of you, in the name of Jesus Christ for the forgiveness of your sins," then, we will "receive the gift of the Holy Spirit" so that "times of refreshing may come from the Lord." (Acts 3:19) This is the promise of the New Testament. This is the repentance and redemption of the new era brought about by Jesus Christ. This is the foundation that built Western civilization, and if our civilization is to survive, we must repent and be baptized.

Our time of refreshing will begin, when on our knees, Western men and women pray, "Christ, forgive me for I have sinned." With this prayer, the desert owl and lonely bird are cut from our hearts. Our sins are forgiven, and like the people of Jerusalem on the Day of Pentecost, we ask, "What shall we do?" The answer that Peter gave two thousand years ago remains the answer for today. We must "be baptized, every one of you, in the name of Jesus Christ for the forgiveness of your sins. And you will receive the gift of the Holy Spirit." (Acts 2:38)

Baptism is the public ceremony and sacrament that physically affirms the repentance in our hearts, but it's more than a ceremony. Something else happens. We receive the gift of the Holy Spirit, and our souls are refreshed. (Acts 3:19) Refreshed by God, our lives are now ready to take on a beautiful new shape. How your new shape is expressed will be unique to you. Perhaps the new shape of your soul makes you kinder, more respectful, and civil – you're simply a happier person. Perhaps, in your new shape, you are a better mother, father, son, daughter, spouse, or neighbor. You see, it's not the big things. It's the small things that reveal the shape of our lives, and lives planted beside God's still water are beautifully shaped, because they conform to God's pattern that is genuine and authentic. This doesn't mean that trouble will never come your way. But it does mean that when trouble comes, you are not alone for your soul no long inhabits the barren spiritual wasteland of the desert owl and lonely bird. Your soul is in a garden with Our Savior, and this is the refreshment of repentance. With this refreshment comes confidence and a new ability. It is the ability to see through phoniness and an unwillingness to participate in it. When enough of us are refreshed, the goodness of our society will return, because we are genuine and authentic people.

Part II: Worship Tells Us Who We Were and Who We Ought To Be

Of Religious Worship and the Sabbath Day

The light of nature showeth that there is a God, who hath lordship and sovereignty over all; is good, and doeth good unto all; and is therefore to be feared, loved, praised, called upon, trusted in, and served with all the heart, and with all the soul, and with all the might.

The Westminster Confession of Faith, Chapter XIII, 6.112.

Chapter 4:
Call to Worship

[8] Then the man and his wife heard the sound of the Lord God as he was walking in the garden in the cool of the day, and they hid from the Lord God among the trees of the garden. [9] But the Lord God called to the man, "Where are you?" [10] He answered, "I heard you in the garden, and I was afraid because I was naked; so I hid." (Genesis 3:8-9)

"Where are you?" Those were the last words that Adam and Eve wanted to hear. They had sinned, and they knew that God knew they had sinned. Yet God called to them, and thus begins the Creator-creature story that is told in the Bible. God's call to humankind is universal and eternal. When we kneel in private prayer or enter the church sanctuary, we are answering God's call saying, "Here I am." With those words, fellowship with God begins. It's not surprising then that the first order of business in the liturgy is the Call to Worship. God's call to fellowship and worship isn't just to individuals. He calls nations and leaders, and Western nations have centuries old ceremonies that are worship services. By participating in these ceremonies, the leader and the people are corporately saying, "Here I am." The story of one of those ceremonies is told here.

* * *

From 1st Century Jerusalem to London, 1953

The school boys had rehearsed for weeks. They were the Queen's Scholars of Westminster School, and the moment of this once in a lifetime performance had arrived. From their places in the choir, the boys stood at attention in their freshly pressed robes, and listened as the processional hymn that filled Westminster Abbey's cavernous nave moved toward the crescendo. It was Coronation Day, and from the corners of their eyes – they dare not turn their heads – they could see their young queen surrounded by her entourage progressing down the center aisle of the packed abbey. Their attention was riveted on the choir director, waiting for their cue. The music lulled. Quickly, with a snap of his wrist, the director pointed, and with all the gusto their young lungs and voices could muster, they sang in glorious acapella unison, "Vivat Regina! Vivat Regina Elizabetha! Vivat! Vivat! Vivat!" Their song raced through the abbey as Elizabeth passed the choir and took her place in the St. Edward Coronation Chair.

Every English monarch since 1296 has sat in St. Edward's chair and waited, as the Archbishop of Canterbury carefully placed the crown on their royal head. Now, in the mid-20th Century, it was Elizabeth's turn. She swore the sovereign's oath, and flawless carried out all the ancient and solemn ceremonies; only one remained. It was the moment when the coronation ceremony required something quite unroyal. Elizabeth stood alone in the abbey's expansive chancel. She was totally exposed. Unlike Eve in the garden, Elizabeth wasn't naked. She was in fact fully clothed, but to her she might as well have been completely undressed. All her royal refinements had been removed. The handstitched, ornately embroidered, golden threaded dress made from the world's finest fabrics had been unclasped and slipped from her slender youthful shoulders. Underneath she wore a simple unadorned short sleeve white linen dress. And, she certainly wasn't hiding. She stood front and center in the abbey and literally, the world was watching. It was June 2, 1953 when she was coronated as Queen Elizabeth the Second, by the Grace of God, Queen of this Realm and of Her Other Realms and Territories, Head of the Commonwealth, and Defender of the Faith. Prime Minster Sir Winston Churchill said, "It was a day which the oldest are proud to have lived to see, and which the youngest will remember all their lives."

The BBC was broadcasting the ceremony live on both radio and TV. Elizabeth's coronation was the first English coronation to be shown on TV, and to ensure that all her subjects witnessed the ceremony, the event was being filmed. In this 1950's pre-satellite era that lacked instant communication, RAF jets stood at the ready to fly the film to all parts of the Commonwealth. Due to the time difference and the speed of new jet planes, Canadians would watch the coronation ceremony that day perhaps in the afternoon, and in Australia, Aussies would view it tomorrow, as would Elizabeth's subjects in Hong Kong. Yet, none of them would witness what would happen next. Only those inside the abbey had the benefit of seeing the most solemn and sacred part of the coronation ceremony, the Anointing of the Holy Spirit. This part of the ceremony was considered too intimate, too personal, and too holy to have cameras intruding.

What a pity that 1950's sensibilities prevented the world from witnessing this moment for what happens in the anointing ceremony reveals the living, beating heart of Western civilization. But, to fully appreciate the Anointing of the Holy Spirit, we need to back up all the way to that moment when Adam and Eve were hiding from God among Eden's trees. From the chancel of Westminster Abbey, we will peer over Elizabeth's shoulder and by looking back in time from the abbey to Eden, we will see the soul of Western civilization and know who we are as a person and people.

It was a desperate moment in Eden. Adam and Eve had disobeyed God, eaten the apple, and now were in hiding. Yet, the passage from Genesis tells us that "he [the Lord God] was walking in the garden in the cool of the day," looking for Adam and Eve. Do we honestly think that God, who is Our Creator, who is omnipotent and omniscient, and who dwells in eternity, really did not know where they were? Of course, he did, and further, he knew what they had done. He knew that the perfect fellowship that he, the Creator, enjoyed with his creatures was now broken, but he stilled called out to Adam and Eve – and by extension all humankind – looking for them. In spite of their sinfulness, he still cared for them. But, Adam and Eve couldn't fellowship with God. Their sin and guilt ended the perfection of Eden's divine relationship. And as a result, the eternity that God had planted in their hearts and that is nourished and sustained through worship of him shrank. There was a void in their souls, where the Lord God's love had been. Sin had removed Our Creator from their hearts and now they were afraid and unable to fellowship with him, worship him, or even face him. So, they did what we all do; they hid. From their hiding place, the story of the Bible begins, which is God's redemption of humankind, i.e., God's restoration of the broken fellowship.

The story unfolds over millennia, and a central character in this human and divine drama is David, who became ancient Israel's greatest king, and from whose lineage, Jesus Christ is descended. David's story begins with God's prophet, Samuel, delivering some very bad news to the sitting king, who was Saul. Samuel told Saul that "your kingdom will not endure," and that "the Lord has sought out a man after his own heart and appointed him ruler of his people." (1 Samuel 13:14). The man, who was "after his [God's] own heart" was David, a shepherd boy, who was the youngest of eight brothers. He was destined to rule and his distinguishing qualification – in fact seemingly his only qualification – for governing and leadership was that his heart desired God's heart. Eternity and worship lived in David.

Under God's direction, Samuel anointed David king, (1 Samuel 16:13), and throughout his turbulent and hard-fought rise to kingship to his building of a great kingdom, we see a strong man, a great leader, and a courageous warrior, as well as a flawed man, who made sinful mistakes and did even more sinful things in a cover-up. Yet, we know through all of David's ups and downs that the defining quality of his character was that his heart desired God's heart. David desired to live his life in the presence of the Living God. We know this because David's thoughts and feelings are so beautifully written by his hand in the Book of Psalms. Hear his words from Psalm 139:

Where can I go from your Spirit?
Where can I flee from your presence?
8 If I go up to the heavens, you are there;
if I make my bed in the depths, you are there.
9 If I rise on the wings of the dawn,
if I settle on the far side of the sea,
10 even there your hand will guide me,
your right hand will hold me fast.
11 If I say, "Surely the darkness will hide me
and the light become night around me,"
12 even the darkness will not be dark to you;
the night will shine like the day,
for darkness is as light to you.

Unlike Adam and Eve, there is not a hint of fear in David's poetic voice. At the end of his life, when he was weakened by age and worn down by insurrection in his own family, David chose his son, Solomon to succeed him. Solomon would be Israel's next king. And, his anointing is recorded in 1 Kings 1 as follows:

So Zadok the priest, Nathan the prophet ... went down and had Solomon mount King David's mule, and they escorted him to Gihon. 39 Zadok the priest took the horn of oil from the sacred tent and anointed Solomon. Then they sounded the trumpet and all the people shouted, "Long live King Solomon!" (1 Kings 1:38-39)

With Solomon's anointing, David's chapter closed, and a new chapter in ancient Israel's story began, but the theme of the story, i.e., the Bible, remained unchanged from the time of Adam and Eve. It was redemption and this redemptive story culminated with the coming of Christ Jesus. The natural response of a redeemed person is that, like David, their heart desires God's heart, and this desire is expressed through worship.

Now Elizabeth, like David and Solomon millennia before, was to be appointed to rule by a man of God. She was only 27 years old. Stripped of all royal trappings, and a wearing a humble linen dress, she prepared to be anointed by Geoffrey Fisher, the Archbishop of Canterbury. For the English, this ceremony dates back to the coronation of King Edgar in 973 at Bath Abbey. Every English monarch for a thousand years has stripped off his or her royal robes, knelt before God, and received the Anointing of the Holy Spirit. Now it was Elizabeth's turn.

She waited as bishops and clergy of the Church of England, each holding a tent pole attached to a yellow canopy lifted it overhead. The archbishop carrying a container of consecrated oil took his place under the canopy that harkens back to the Tabernacle of the Exodus. The Tabernacle was a tent that moved with the Children of Israel throughout their long journey in the Sinai Desert. More importantly, it was the dwelling place of God on earth, and wherever the Israelites camped, the Tabernacle would be set up in the center. The tents of families would be arrayed around the Tabernacle, and therefore, God himself was at the center of Israelite society. The yellow canopy under which the archbishop waited for Elizabeth is a reminder that God is at the center of the nation's life.

As Elizabeth entered the canopy, the cameras cut away. Therefore, no pictures or footage of the anointing of Elizabeth are known to be publicly available. We do know, however, from the firsthand description on radio that the archbishop applied the holy oil to her head, hands, and heart. With each anointing, he traced the sign of the cross in the oil. Head, hands, and heart were marked with the cross of Christ. As sovereign, her thoughts, actions, and desires were under Christ and were to reflect Christ's life and teaching so that God might tabernacle, i.e., dwell, in the center of the nation. Just as blood flows to the heart to be oxygenated and regenerated to give life to the body, the Anointing of the Holy Spirit reveals the beating heart of Western civilization and source of our life and regeneration. It is Christ who is – or sadly perhaps was – at the center of the West's foundational story.

The ceremony complete, the cameras returned, and showed Elizabeth donning a splendid yellow robe, as the resounding notes of Handel's "Zadok, the Priest" filled the abbey. The choir joined in singing:

Zadok the Priest, and Nathan the
Prophet anointed Solomon King.
And all the people rejoiced, and said:
God save the King! Long live the King!
May the King live forever,
Amen, Alleluia.

Sadly, most Westerners are totally unaware of the deep and profound Christian roots found, not only in English coronations, but in all coronation ceremonies for Western monarchs. Such ignorance is like moths eating away at the ancient fabric that binds society together, and that is exactly how too many see Western society – old, worn out, and eaten away with ugly gaping holes. However, once made aware of the

West's Christian roots, the response is too often cynicism. Regarding the coronation ceremony: the cynicism is expressed in terms of acquisition of power; as in, the Bible and Christianity are only props used to provide an air of legitimacy to the king or queen. Likewise, when presidents, prime ministers, members of parliament, senators, congressmen, and governors are sworn into office on the Bible and the ceremony is accompanied by prayer, the modern harsh criticism is the same – these are merely props that lack any relevance today.

Such a view is partially accurate. Coronations and swearing in ceremonies, including anointings, are for the purpose of establishing legitimacy to rule. But, to think of these ceremonies only in terms of authority, power, and legitimacy reveals the corruption of modern minds and misses the fundamental point entirely: how do these ceremonies legitimize rulers? They legitimize, because they are true expressions of what society believes, or at least once believed. The ceremonies are a retelling of the foundational story, and in the case of the West, our story is Christian. Because we are Christian nations, all rulers from kings and queens, presidents to prime ministers, and mayors to city councilpersons must at least appear to exercise their authority within the narrative of the West's foundational story. What the modern cynics really don't like about Christian coronations and swearing in ceremonies is that they constrain power, and 21st Century atheist progressive intellectuals crave power. The West's Christian foundational story thwarts them in their godless pursuit.

How Christianity constrains power is on full display in the English coronation ceremony. Before being crowned, Elizabeth swore an oath to govern mercifully under the rule of law and within the guidance provided by scripture and the Church of England. This oath encompassed governing with justice and integrity. While not stated in the coronation, the source of morality, virtue, integrity, justice, and mercy are the Ten Commandments and Jesus' Sermon on the Mount. These are the millennia-old founding documents of Western governments and law, and they constrain the power of rulers, because they teach that God is the ultimate sovereign and each us – even rulers – have a moral responsibility to others.

Such biblical teaching was once so thoroughly inculcated into Western hearts and minds that it was unnecessary to acknowledge them as the source of our freedoms, but like moths eating away ancient fabric, we see there are ragged gaps in biblical knowledge today and gaping holes in our foundational story as illustrated by Charles, the Prince of Wales, who is next in line for the English throne.

One of the titles of English monarchs is "Defender of the Faith." If or when Charles takes the throne to reign as King Charles III, he has expressed reluctance to assume this title. His reluctance reveals the core of a pernicious and deep Western problem. The coronation oath requires him to swear to "maintain the Laws of God and the true profession of the Gospel." The basis of this oath is that truth comes from God and scripture, and by swearing to it, the new monarch is affirming that God is source of all truth and all law, including British Common Law. If you are reluctant to be identified as "Defender of the Faith," because there are many faiths and therefore many truths, you certainly cannot swear that truth comes from God and the Gospels. Charles', and by extension a large percentage of Westerners', reluctance, inability, or sheer cowardice to affirm God and scripture as the source of truth tears at our foundational story, creates confusion, and threatens freedom. Meanwhile, those hungry for power wait and hope that Western sleepers, like Prince Charles, never awake to what's really at stake. Elizabeth foreshadowed as far back as

1953 on Coronation Day that one day our foundational story might be in peril.

With the pomp, pageantry, and splendor of royal parades over and the coronation ceremony in the abbey completed, a very tired Elizabeth returned to Buckingham Palace. But, she had one last duty to perform that day. She had to address her subjects. The BBC had prepared the microphones and cameras. Elizabeth took a seat behind a desk and said:

The ceremonies you have seen today are ancient, and some of their origins are veiled in the mist of the past. But, their spirit and their meaning shine through the ages never perhaps more brightly than now.

Elizabeth was not yet 30 when these words were broadcast worldwide from Buckingham Palace. As her words raced to the most remote parts of the Commonwealth, Londoners filled the palace's broad plaza, and pressed against its gilded gates, hoping for a glimpse of their sovereign. When she appeared on a balcony and gave her now ionic little wave of the hand, the throng cheered wildly.

Sixty-seven years have passed since Coronation Day, and the young queen is now an elderly lady of 94. If in 1953 the origins of the coronation ceremony were veiled and misty, what are they today? Cloaked? Obscured? Tarnished? Forgotten? And, what of the underlying meaning and spirit that the ceremony is intended to convey? The young Elizabeth was hopeful that their significance shined brightly. Looking at her subjects today, including her own son, the Prince of Wales, does she remain hopeful that the spirit of coronation still shines in the hearts and minds of the British people? More importantly, what was that shining spirit?

It was the spirit of home bound together by the shared experience of queen and subject responding to God's call to worship. It was a spirit that said: the Lord God is our God, this land is our home, and this is who we are as a people. It was the spirit of hope that came from a shared faith in a Savior, Jesus Christ and through this shared faith and mutual hope came shared values and a mutual destiny both in this life and the next. It was the spirit of a people who were not afraid. This was the story of their home, and it imparted meaning to personal lives and to the life of a nation.

Intrinsic to being human is the need for meaning. Symbols, ceremonies, songs, and stories are the most significant avenues by which societies, religions, and families communicate meaning. All cultures from primitive tribes isolated deep in the Amazon rainforest to the wealthiest, most technologically advanced nations have traditions that brim with symbols, storytelling, ceremonies, and depending upon the culture songs and musical instruments. Society's foundational story is what is being communicated, and the coronation ceremony tells us volumes about how, not only the British people, but the West in general identifies itself. We are Christians, who worship the resurrected Savoir, Jesus Christ. He is the cornerstone of our foundational story, and our story is not a fossilized historical artifact, as those in opposition to it would like us to believe. The West's story is actually faith that is put into practice, and we see evidence of the story in what the West does, as the following list illustrates:

Why are we in the West so concerned with the environment and sustainability? Because God made humankind stewards of it.

Why are we in the West so concerned with human rights? Because God planted eternity in our hearts; we are eternal creatures created in the image of God with rights imparted from Him.

Why has the West led the world in scientific and technical achievements that have raised the standard of living worldwide? Because God gave all of Nature to humankind and told us to name it, enjoy it, be fruitful and multiply it.

Why does the West take in refugees and why do we feed the poor around the world? Because God told us to tend to the least among us, and that we are our brother's keeper.

Why does the West intervene to end wars, when it is not in our interest to become involved? Because Jesus said, "Blessed are the peacemakers, for they will be called the children of God." (Matthew 5:9)

Politics, economics, and national power, of course, come into play in each of these initiatives that are so characteristic of the West. However, before a discourse on politics, economics, and projection of national power can begin, there must be a societal consensus that the West's initiatives are at least acceptable, if not good and beneficial. The source of our understanding of what is acceptable, good, and beneficial comes directly from our foundational story that is overwhelmingly Christian.

Because the West has so embraced Christianity, no other nations on earth have achieved so much and done so much to advance liberty and human welfare than the nations of the West. This statement in no way means that the West "owns" Christianity for the redemption and fellowship with God that comes through Jesus Christ is for all nations, all races, and all people. What happened in the West was that men and women answered God's call to worship, and over a two-thousand-year history Christianity became rooted in our culture, and in doing so became the core of our foundational story. That story is told in worship through our symbols, ceremonies, songs, and stories. It is our inheritance. It is who we were. It is our home.

Further, because Western nations are Christian does not mean that people of other faiths cannot live and thrive among us. In fact, it's just the opposite. Because we are Christians and are secure in our faith and knowledge that God and scripture is the source of all truth, Western society can and does accommodate citizens of other faiths, and no other nations on earth are so welcoming. In fact, religious, tribal, and economic persecution around the world drives people to the West in search of sanctuary, and sanctuary exists in the West, because it is part of our Christian foundational story. If sanctuary is to continue and our freedoms to endure, then the continual tearing down of the West's foundational story must stop, because if left unchecked, our story dies and with it our freedoms and also our goodness; it dies too. Once our faith is dead, the world becomes a very dark place indeed!

Like people and societies, a foundational story is a living entity. It must be nourished and propagated, which means that the story must be retold on a regular basis so that the ideals of the story inspire a living into it. For the West, Sabbath worship is where the retelling and inspiration happen. A royal coronation is at best a once in a lifetime event. Therefore, a royal anointing is an event that most people will never see. Yet anointings and a related ceremony of "laying on hands" that involves no use of consecrated oil occurs routinely in churches. Before assuming leadership roles, priests, pastors, elders, and deacons are appointed to lead by either anointing and/or laying on of hands. The ill and infirmed are often anointed in healing services. It's what Christians have done for two thousand years! Weekly Sabbath worship is where the roots of our foundational story are propagated and nourished, and a coronation or swearing in ceremony is like a blossom that occurs only on special occasions. But for the flower to bloom, the root system must be intact and healthy. Otherwise, the plant, i.e., the story, dies, and the flower fades and withers. Therefore, both as a person and a people, answering God's call to worship is immensely important. In fact, our lives, nations, and eternity hinge upon it. We must not be like Adam and Eve. We must through faith in Christ put aside our fears, step out of hiding, and say, "Here I am, Lord. Like David, my heart desires your heart." This is how our story will live, and how answering the call to worship restores us.

"Where are you?"

"Here I am, Lord."

Chapter 5:
Confession of Sin & Assurance of Pardon

"Woman, where are they? Has no one condemned you?"
11 "No one, sir," she said.
"Then neither do I condemn you," Jesus declared. "Go now and leave your life of sin" (John 8:10-11)

This passage from John is the dramatic conclusion to a life-and-death situation that happened in the Temple courtyard. A woman, who the scriptures say was "caught in adultery," was drug by a mob to the Temple, where Jesus was teaching. The Temple authorities demanded that Jesus judge her. The verses above are his judgment and sentence, which were, "Go now and leave your life of sin." This attempt at mob justice teaches us much about sin, forgiveness, and pardon. More importantly, it reveals who Jesus is.

When the unnamed woman was drug before Jesus, her only hope was that Jesus' judgment would be merciful. After all, there was no doubt of her guilt. But, she received so much more than mercy; she received pardon. She received the grace of Christ Jesus, who has the power to forgive our sins. She walked away a free woman, and this is the part that Western men and women have trouble accepting and understanding. Through our faith in him, Jesus forgives our sins. We are free of them; we don't have haul them around with us like a heavy backpack weighing us down. When we confess our sins, we have assurance of pardon.

We are now going to travel back in time to Nazi occupied France where we will meet three very sinful people. They are fictional, but these characters along with the writer, who created them, offer great insight into how the Western intellectual, philosophical class understand Christianity, sin, and judgment.

With what we learned in mind, we will return to the scripture passage of the woman caught in adultery to see how Jesus Christ really deals with sin, mercy, grace, and pardon. Before we begin our journey, a word of caution is needed. The behavior of the fictional characters is appalling, even shocking. Like the woman caught in adultery and brought to Jesus, these characters did things that decent people don't talk about. But, let's not allow the sins to obscure the soul of the sinner. That's what the mob did in dragging the poor woman to the Temple courtyard, but Jesus saw her soul and forgave her. When we can see souls and not just sins, we better understand the power of Christ's forgiveness in our own lives. Now, let's begin our journey.

* * *

From 1st Century Jerusalem to Paris, 1944

The Metro still ran. Cars and buses still filled the boulevards and circled the Arc de Triomphe. Parisians still lingered in sidewalk cafes. Cabarets still entertained, and at night thousands of lights still cast their magical spell giving Paris its signature name, the City of Lights. The Parisian spirit, however, was shuttered, cloistered, and in hiding. France had been occupied by the Nazis for four years. The war was not going well for Germany, but liberation remained a dream rather than a promise kept. People lived in a meta-state, suspended between the dream and the promise fulfilled. They were living yet not alive, and they did not know when, or if, their purgatory would end.

Jean-Paul Sartre, the existentialist philosopher, novelist, playwright, and social activist, lived this meta-state existence, and during the Nazi occupation, he wrote a one-act play entitled, *Huis Clos* (No Exit). It debuted in Paris at the Théâtre du Vieux-Colombier in May 1944. The play was not a political manifesto. German censors would never have allowed such a play to open. Rather, *Huis Clos* was a journey into the human heart and a weighing of the consequences that spring from the heart's dark corners.

Three actors occupy the stage. Joseph Garcin, Inès Serrano, and Estelle Rigualt are dead and newly arrived in hell. Each imagines with dread the torture and horrors that await. One-by-one, first Joseph, then Inès, and finally Estelle are led by a hotel valet, not to a demon-filled furnace, but to a sitting room furnished with heavy, ornate, and out of fashion Second Empire style furniture. They all find the furniture distasteful, but to Estelle, it was especially ghastly. She was horrified that the green sofa on which she will sit forever clashes with her vibrant red dress, and she knows that there is not a moment's relief from this assault on her sense of style and fashion. This hideous salon is the only room. There is not even a bathroom, because as the valet tells them, the dead don't need to brush their teeth or bother with any personal hygiene. Even blinking is a thing of the past. As the door closes behind the valet – a door whose threshold they know they will never again cross – they wonder at the type of hell that awaits.

Politely, they introduce themselves and greet one another. They agree that since they will be together forever, they should get to know each other. Joseph explains that in life he was a writer, journalist, and pacifist. War was repugnant to him, and courageously he campaigned against it. His views found expression in a newspaper that he and his friends zealously published. However, his pacifist crusade cost him his life. He was arrested, and sentenced to death by firing squad, which he says he faced bravely and without regret, because even staring at death, he would not cower and renounce his principles.

Inès' story is less dramatic. In life she was a Parisian postal worker, who made ends meet by living with her cousin and his wife, Florence. She provided few details regarding her life, and did not mention how she died. She hinted, however, that the living arrangement with her cousin and his wife was satisfactory, and that the three of them got along well together, living humble and simple lives.

Estelle too says she was a good person. While alive, her primary focus was the welfare of her younger brother. He had special needs. She did not specify what those were, saying only that their family was desperately poor and the care he required was unaffordable. For the sake of her brother, Estelle married a wealthy man, who was five times her age. She sacrificed a potential loving and fulfilling marriage to a younger man to ensure that her brother received proper care. Surprisingly, she said that the first five years of marriage were good, but with time, the marriage faltered yet she remained faithful to her husband for the sake of her brother. It was her duty. Estelle said that she died of pneumonia in her home and at peace.

Their life stories emerge haltingly and amid constant bickering. They complain of the stifling hot room, which only adds to the tension. As they probe and assess, parry and thrust one another, their true natures are revealed. Estelle is immensely vain and narcissistic. She laments that she does not have a mirror to check her make-up. Inès uses Estelle's vanity as an opening to make sexual advances, revealing that she is a lesbian. Estelle rebuffs Inès' advances, and turns to Joseph to affirm her own beauty and sex appeal to a man. He rejects her, and Estelle attempts to wound him by saying that in life he was no crusader for peace, but simply a coward.

As their fighting escalates, they reveal that the life stories they told are merely fanciful interpretations of the realities that sent them to hell. Bit-by-bit, their true stories emerge, and with each new revelation they tear into one another. They try to make peace, but cannot. It is then they realize that they were not randomly assigned to this room. There is purpose behind the three of them being together. That purpose is to torture one another. The character, personality, and sins that are unique to each person are the instrument of torture for the others. In this bitter and charged atmosphere, they tell who they really were in life.

Joseph was no man of courage and principle. He was not even a pacifist. He was a deserter from his unit in wartime. He was able to hop a train and escape the battlefield, but he was caught and returned. After a trial, he was executed by a firing squad. Cowardice, however, was not his only character flaw. He was a perverse and cruel womanizer, bedding young women in his own home in front of wife. He said he wreaked of cigars, whiskey, and sex, and that he caused his gentle wife much pain. A weak, wicked, and cowardly man, he tells Estelle that he will have sex with her, if only she will say that he is a faithful and courageous man. If she will say these things, he believes he can find relief, if not salvation. She refuses, and his despair deepens.

In her hunt for Estelle's affection, Inès tells her true story. She took advantage of the close living arrangement with her cousin and his wife. She seduced Florence, who fully succumbed to Inès' desires. This betrayal, not to another man but to a woman who was his cousin, was too much for Florence's husband. He intentionally stepped in front of an oncoming train. His suicide had further tragic consequences. One night overcome by guilt, Florence rose from the bed she shared with Inès, and turned on a gas stove. By morning, they were both dead. Now in hell, Inès is racked by lust and jealously, as she watches Estelle's attempts to seduce Joseph. In her anger and despair, she too taunts him as a coward.

Now, vain Estelle's true story tumbles out. She was no saintly sister, caring solely for her special needs brother, while doting on her elderly husband. She was as promiscuous as a stray cat. She became pregnant by Roger, one of her many lovers. Her husband's wealth allowed she and Roger to travel to Switzerland, during the final months of her pregnancy. There, Estelle delivered a healthy baby girl, a child she never intended to keep. Only days after the birth, she threw her newborn daughter into a lake, drowning her. Overcome with guilt and grief, Roger shot himself in the face and died. Seemingly unfazed, Estelle returned home to Paris, and proceeded to bed more men, including an 18-year-old, whom she longs for in hell. But, in hell there is only Joseph and he refuses her. Estelle did die of pneumonia, but she wasn't at peace.

With their true stories out and in the knowledge that they are each other's torturers for eternity, Joseph screams, "HELL IS OTHER PEOPLE!" When he regains his composure, Sartre cleverly ends the play with Joseph calmly saying, "Eh bien, continuons." (Oh well, let's continue.)

The curtain soon closed on *Huis Clos*, and on the Nazi occupation of France, as well. Paris was liberated the year following the play's debut. In the post-war period, Sartre published, among other books, *Existentialism is a Humanism* (1946). Today, the meaning and value of Sartre's existentialism is debated by philosophers, and *Huis Clos* is a lightly regarded play. These views of Sartre and *Huis Clos*, however, are of no consequence here, because the purpose of offering a detailed summary of the play was not to delve into existentialism, but to glimpse into the souls of Sartre's characters, take note of the hell he created for them, and ask questions. Is the hell that Sartre imagined the real life that Westerners live today? Like Joseph, Inès, and Estelle, who were dead, are we trapped alive in a life that has no hope, no forgiveness, no pardon, and no redemption? Like Sartre's characters, are we angry – angry at life because there is no exit, angry with each other, and angry with ourselves yet all the while inexplicably celebrating our carnal selves, our narcissistic selves, our unfeeling selves, and our lying selves?

Regrettably, the hell that Sartre imagined is real life for millions of Westerners. Certainly, the sins in *Huis Clos* are the same as we commit today, differing only perhaps in degree. Joseph, Inès, and Estelle were carnal, lusting, selfish, narcissistic, unfeeling, prideful, and lying souls, but there is nothing new here. These sins have defined the human condition since pride and lies prompted Adam and Eve to defy God. What is new today is that these sins are celebrated. Sartre, who died in 1980, could not have imagined that in the 21st Century the behavior of his characters would be viewed as unremarkable, and seen as nothing more than the free expression of sexuality among consenting adults. This is a fundamental change in the West's millennia-old understanding of Judeo-Christian morality that today is viewed as outdated and even mean. Whether or not the West's past moral code is outdated and mean is an ongoing debate, but what is undeniable is that rejection of it has created the walls of the West's hell.

When Sartre wrote *Huis Clos* in the mid-20th Century, belief in a Divine Judge, who rightly judges individuals at their death was a Western consensus. This point is reinforced by Sartre's own beliefs. Ironically, Sartre was a Marxist atheist yet he called himself a "Catholic atheist," and the influence of the church on *Huis Clos* is unmistakable. The unstated assumption upon which the whole play turns is that Joseph, Inès, and Estelle were righteously judged and deserved hell. They never questioned their punishment. Today, with atheism so prevalent, and biblical knowledge essentially nonexistent, the traditional consensus regarding the truth of God, sin, judgment, punishment, redemption, and salvation are gone, and replaced by a consensus that there is no truth. Therefore, any viewpoint concerning how life is to be lived – no matter how wacky – is acceptable save one. The Christian viewpoint that proclaims truth comes from God is entirely unacceptable, and as a consequence an effort is underway in the West to expunge the understanding that truth comes from God. The walls of our hell were built by our rejection of Judeo-Christian morality, and the door of our prison room was locked by our denial of truth.

Like Parisians in Nazi occupied France, our prison room traps Westerners in a meta-state existence. We know the existence we live is not what we want, yet we are frozen, trapped in our meta-state, and unwilling or unable to change it. Worse, we are also like Joseph, Inès, and Estelle. We are sinful, and we see the destruction of sin in our lives, the lives of our friends and family, and in the life of our society. We cannot deny that Western society is increasingly coarse, banal, obscene, cruel, and violent, but we don't vigorously push back against it. Instead, we dither and vacillate, not wanting to offend or appear old fashioned. Such is the meta-state of our existence! We are suspended, motionless, and locked by sin in our prison room, where we are tortured by the feeling that on the other side of our prison door, there actually is truth, but we are afraid to approach the door and try the knob. What if it actually opened? What if there really is a righteous God, who judges our sins? We don't dare open that door! Better to remain in our prison cell of sin and deception than risk encountering the Lord God Almighty. The West truly exists in a meta-state, where we are alive, but not living!

Here is the West's true tragedy: we do know what's on the other side of the door. It is Jesus Christ, Our Savior, who waits to forgive our sins. Christ's compassion, mercy, love, empathy, forgiveness and redemption were on full display when the unnamed woman (perhaps her name was Estelle) was caught in adultery, and drug by a mob to the vast open courtyard of the Temple in Jerusalem to where Jesus was teaching. The passage in John the eighth chapter says, "The teachers of the law and the Pharisees ... made her stand before the group and [they] said to Jesus, "Teacher, this woman was caught in the act of adultery. In the Law, Moses commanded us to stone such women. Now what do you say?"

Jesus didn't answer. Instead, he bent down and began writing with his finger in the dust and dirt of the courtyard. It would be fascinating to know what he wrote, but the gospels offer not even a hint. While he was writing, the men, who held her, taunted Jesus, trying to get him to judge and condemn her, when in fact, as teachers of the law, it was their job to pass judgment and assign punishment. But, dragging her before Jesus and the crowd around him was all part of their twisted plot. They hoped to trap Jesus. What judgment would he render with his followers watching? Forgive her, and he's not keeping the law; condemn her to death, then maybe he doesn't really have the power to forgive sins. Therefore, her accusers waited with malicious anticipation, as they watched him write in the dust.

The scriptures tells us that after a few moments Jesus "straightened up and said to them, *"Let any one of you who is without sin be the first to throw a stone at her." [8] Again he stooped down and wrote on the ground. [9] At this, those who heard began to go away one at a time, the older ones first, until only Jesus was left, with the woman still standing there. [10] Jesus straightened up and asked her, "Woman, where are they? Has no one condemned you?"*

[11] "No one, sir," she said.

"Then neither do I condemn you," Jesus declared. "Go now and leave your life of sin."

It's a powerful story. Without saying a word, Jesus judged the woman's judges, and in the process, avoided a clever trap, but there's even more to this story. This unfortunate, humiliated woman was brought before a type of court that thankfully doesn't exist in the modern West. It was a religious court with secular power and the authority to carry out even death sentences. In this sacred-secular court, she stood in the docket of the accused and Jesus was her only hope, and he did not fail her. He was her advocate and compassionate judge, who understood her, forgave her, and commuted her sentence. She received a full pardon.

We owe the teachers of the Law and Pharisees, who devised this trap, our gratitude. In their malevolent zeal to entrap Jesus, they inadvertently reveal who he really is. He is our advocate, who empathizes with us, who has compassion on us, who judges us with mercy, and who has the power to forgive all of our sins and grant us grace. Jesus is qualified to serve as advocate and judge with the power to pardon and the authority offer grace, because he is the Son of God, and the Son of Man. Both terms apply, and he used the latter, Son of Man, often when referring to himself. Christians hold that Jesus is fully human, and thus able to empathize with us and advocate for us, and fully God with the authority to judge and forgive us. His death and resurrection demonstrates both his humanity and his divinity. Therefore, we look to Jesus for forgiveness and pardon of our sins.

The scriptures assure us that when we confess our sins and repent of them, Jesus pardons us. Repent means to stop, turn around, and head in the opposite direction. That is exactly what Jesus commanded the adulterous woman do, when he said, "Go now and leave your life of sin." In Sartre's world of atheistic humanism, that so afflicts the West today, there is no hope of forgiveness, pardon, and redemption, because there is no God and there is no truth. Here is the choice that Western men and women face today. Do we stay in this prison room with Sartre, and eternally torture each other with our sin, guilt, recrimination, and accusations even as we lust after each other? Or, do we turn the knob of our prison door and open it?

The obstacles that freeze us in our meta-state of inaction are so transparently feeble! Are Western men and women really going to allow a 20th Century, haughty, pseudo-intellectual, atheistic, relativistic humanism exemplified by a Marxist existentialist philosopher prevent us from turning the knob to see if there is way out? So far, the answer is yes, because we don't want to appear ignorant, backwards, and science-deniers, and we certainly don't want to be accused of being a Christian. The chains that bind our hearts and minds are so flimsy it's embarrassing to call them chains! Here is the truth: we want to turn that knob. We want that door to open. We want there to be hope, forgiveness, pardon, redemption, fellowship with God, and new life. We want these things because Our Creator has made us in his image, and God's creation is good. It's not evil. The first chapter of Genesis tells us repeatedly that all of creation – all of life – abounds with God's goodness. The mightiest act of God's goodness is Our Savior, who restores the goodness that was placed in our hearts at Creation. It's the way we are made, and the basis for four thousand years of Judeo-Christian thought. Jesus Christ does wait on the other side of the door, and we only need faith to open it.

When confess our sins, either in private or in the sanctuary, we are turning the knob of our prison door. Once opened, we are as free as the woman that Jesus pardoned. Hear Our Savior's words again.

"Woman, where are they? Has no one condemned you?"

11 "No one, sir," she said.

"Then neither do I condemn you," Jesus declared. "Go now and leave your life of sin"

When we confess our sins, our pardon is assured.

Chapter 6: Pastoral Prayer

What an event it must have been! King Solomon's dedication of the Temple in ancient Jerusalem around 930 BCE was an event for the ages. For the ancient Hebrews, the Temple was the dwelling place of God on earth. The Ark of the Covenant, the menorah, the incense altar, and all the other implements of worship were housed in the Temple. For approximately 300 years, since the Exodus from Egypt, worship had taken place in the Tabernacle, which was the tent that moved with the Israelites as they journeyed across the Sinai Desert. Now, Solomon had completed an impressive Temple that would be the focal point of the nation's worship. The magnitude of the dedication ceremony cannot be overstated. Even today some two thousand and six hundred years since the Babylonians destroyed Solomon's Temple in 586 BCE, the place in Jerusalem where the Temple was built is still called the Temple Mount.

For the dedication ceremony, Solomon summoned all the priests, elders, and leaders of families to Jerusalem. After sacrifices were offered, the priests installed the Ark of the Covenant in the Holy of Holies. And "then Solomon stood before the altar of the Lord in front of the whole assembly of Israel, spread out his hands toward heaven," and gave the dedication prayer. (1 Kings 8:22) The following are excerpts of Solomon's lengthy prayer:

"Lord, the God of Israel, there is no God like you in heaven above or on earth below—you who keep your covenant of love with your servants who continue wholeheartedly in your way.

Hear from heaven, your dwelling place, and when you hear, forgive.

...then hear from heaven and act.

...then hear from heaven and forgive the sin of your people.

...then hear from heaven, your dwelling place. Forgive and act; deal with everyone according to all they do, since you know their hearts (for you alone know every human heart).

...then hear from heaven and forgive the sin of your servants, your people Israel. Teach them the right way to live, and send rain on the land you gave your people for an inheritance.

...then hear from heaven their prayer and their plea, and uphold their cause.

54 When Solomon had finished all these prayers and supplications to the Lord, he rose from before the altar of the Lord, where he had been kneeling with his hands spread out toward heaven. 55 He stood and blessed the whole assembly of Israel in a loud voice, saying:

56 "Praise be to the Lord, who has given rest to his people Israel just as he promised. (Verses excerpted from 1 Kings 8:22-56)

Solomon's prayer is like a hymn. It has stanzas and a refrain. Each stanza highlights a problem of the human condition – sinful behavior, lack of rain for crops, attack by a foreign power, citizens held captive in a distant land, a plea for mercy, and a desire for justice and wisdom. The refrain always begins with "then hear" which is followed by a request for action that includes forgiving, teaching, sending of rain, blessing, and judging. Hear and act are the petitions of Solomon's prayer.

Though ancient, the message of the prayer is timeless, because for three thousand years and continuing to this day, the same prayer has flown to heaven: hear, O Lord and act. Hear our heartaches, fears, illnesses, troubles – hear all the sufferings of life – and act; rescue us! Through the centuries, kings, queens, presidents, and prime ministers have publicly prayed for their nations and people in times of trouble, asking God to hear and to act. Pastors and priests gather their flocks weekly and pray the same prayer: hear, O Lord and act. Never is this prayer a demand. It is always a plea that is offered with heads bowed, hearts humbled, and spirits hopeful, and woven into the prayer is acknowledgement of the Lord God as sovereign over all things.

This is pastoral prayer, and it is offered by a people, who share a common faith and through that faith strive toward a common destiny. On this road toward their common destiny there are stopping points that are the objects of their pastoral prayer. These stopping points are the things about which they are beseeching God to hear and petitioning him to act, and God may or may grant their petitions. That is his sovereign right, and the prospect that God might not act on our behalf exactly as we desire, reveals the foundation of pastoral prayer which is trust in his promises.

God never promised that the destiny he has charted would include our stopping points, i.e., the objectives, the outcomes that we want. However, he did promise that he would never abandon us and that he would bring us to the final destination of prayer which is eternity, the dwelling place of God. Arriving at this destination is not a matter of petitioning God. It is a matter of faith and trust. With life's final destination set as a promise, we make our petitions known to God, and journey life's road in the confidence that whatever outcomes lie ahead, God is with us. This bonding of God and a people in prayer propels a godly society forward, working, achieving, struggling, and thriving in defeat and victory, where all is set within the context of trusting Our Sovereign God. Even while our prayers are yet to be answered, we praise God for the goodness of his promises, and reach across the millennia to join with King Solomon saying, "Praise be to the Lord, who has given rest to his people Israel just as he promised." Like the Children of Israel, God gives us rest in pastoral prayer.

In the section below, the greatest testing of Western civilization is recounted through the lens of pastoral prayer. In the 1930's and '40's, presidents, prime ministers, and kings of Western nations, like Solomon, bowed in humble pastoral prayer, lifting up to God the petitions of their people. We will begin the story at the end of the great testing. Peace reigns, wounds are healing, sorrows are fading, and justice is reestablished. From this blessed endpoint of answered prayer, we will journey back in time to places of such fear and danger that it shook the souls of powerful men, who in their desperate hours humbled themselves and prayed to the Almighty God to deliver us from evil. Years passed before their prayers were answered, but it finally happened in 1945. To put our story in perspective, we will make one final stop at place of unanswered prayers. Now, let's step back in time.

* * *

From 1st Century Jerusalem to Nuremberg, 1946

Solemnly, the eight judges – one each and one alternate from the Allied powers of the United States, Great Britain, France, and the Soviet Union – entered the packed courtroom and took their seats at the bench of justice. In the back of the courtroom, cameramen adjusted the lens of bulky movie cameras. All nations of the world knew that history was taking place in this courtroom. No witness, no legal argument, no outburst, no ruling from the bench – nothing was to go unrecorded. With a rap of the gavel, the courtroom fell silent and came to order. Everyone watched as a US Army officer rose from his chair.

Trim and fit in a neatly pressed uniform with his tie tightly cinched and his hair carefully parted and slicked down, Telford Taylor, Brigadier General of the United States Army stood at the lectern of the Nuremberg courtroom to deliver the prosecution's opening statement in the trial of 23 Nazis. Producing courtroom evidence of crimes did not require an attorney of General Taylor's rank. The evidence was overwhelming, and a junior officer could have presented a compelling case for the prosecution. There were, however, larger moral and ethical issues at stake, and these turned on two questions that are asked in the third and fourth chapters of Genesis: who is God and am I my brother's keeper? With this weight on his shoulders, the general leaned toward the microphone and began.

The victims of these crimes are numbered in the hundreds of thousands. A handful only are still alive; a few of the survivors will appear in this courtroom. But most of these miserable victims were slaughtered outright or died in the course of the tortures to which they were subjected. For the most part they are nameless dead. To their murderers, these wretched people were not individuals at all.[11]

The Nazis on trial were no ordinary men. They were doctors, medical researchers, and highly respected members of the German scientific community that was considered among the best in the world. Some possessed international reputations, having presented scientific papers before the Royal Society in London. Most had sworn the Hippocratic Oath of medical professionals to do no harm. Now they were on trial for their lives, having been the architects of the Nazis' infamous program of "racial hygiene," where non-Nordic peoples such as Jews, gypsies, Slavs, and other ethnicities were deemed inferior and not worthy of living. But race and ethnicity were only one aspect of this all-encompassing program. Homosexuals, the mentally and physically handicapped, the old and infirmed, and any individual or group thought to be a drain on the robustness of the German spirit called *Geist* were targeted for one or all of the following: sterilization, medical experimentation, slave labor, or execution.

The Nazis' racial hygiene program, aimed at ridding the world of these "useless lives," consisted of three primary initiatives.[12] First was the 1933 Sterilization Law that allowed "the involuntary sterilization of anyone suffering a disease thought to be genetically determined, including feeble-mindedness, schizophrenia, manic depressive disorder, epilepsy, Huntington chorea, congenital blindness or deafness, malformation, and severe alcoholism."[13] Before the Nazi madness was brought to an end between 350,000 and 400,000 individuals, or roughly 1% of the population, were forcibly sterilized. Second were the Nuremberg Laws that revoked German citizenship from Jews, and prohibited marriage and any sexual relations between Jews and non-Jews. Third were the laws and policies relating to euthanasia and medical practice. These provided the so-called legal framework – more accurately the cover – under which the Nazi extermination machine operated. Some of the first victims were 5,000 children who were starved to death, died of exposure in unheated wards, or died by injection of poison or chemical warfare agents. But this was only the beginning, before the war's end, the blood of millions of "useless lives" would soak Europe's soil, and these 23 men stood in the courtroom dock accused of unimaginably horrific crimes.

General Taylor continued his opening remarks saying:

The defendants in the dock are charged with murder, but this is no mere murder trial. We cannot rest content when we have shown that crimes were committed and that certain persons committed them. To kill, to maim, and to torture is criminal under all modern systems of law. These defendants did not kill in hot blood, nor for personal enrichment. Some of them may be sadists who killed and tortured for sport, but they are not all perverts. They are not ignorant men. Most of them are trained physicians and some of them are distinguished scientists. Yet these defendants, all of whom were fully able to comprehend the nature of their acts, and most of whom were exceptionally qualified to form a moral and professional judgment in this respect, are responsible for wholesale murder and unspeakably cruel tortures. It is our deep obligation to all peoples of the world to show why and how these things happened.

The stakes were high. The world was watching. Moral and legal precedents would be set in this trial. Through documents, photographs, and heartbreaking testimonies of victims, General Taylor presented the United States' case against these doctors and scientists. When it all was done and the verdicts were read, seven were sentenced to death by hanging, seven were acquitted, and the remainder received long prison sentences during which many of them died.[14]

In 1946, the ashes of war in Europe glowed hot. The evenness, orderliness, and rational thoroughness of General Taylor's opening courtroom statement was a prayerful respite from the chaotic, evil insanity that had convulsed Europe for more than a decade. His words cooled the ashes of war; this was not about revenge. Justice would be done in this trial that was "no mere murder trial." The Doctors' Trial, however, was also no mere murder trial, because it was the application of Judeo-Christian justice to the deeper questions that had set the Nazi insanity in motion: who is God and am I my brother's keeper?

The trial and convictions of these educated, medical, and scientific men answered these deeper questions. The answers are these. You learned men are not gods. You do not get to choose who lives, who dies, who is human and who is not. Your so-called modern science-based hierarchy of human worth, e.g., racial hygiene, is not science at all, but merely a modern version of ancient idolatry. What you called science was really evil hearts unconstrained by God, who says that only he is the sovereign Lord God Almighty, and that because he made all people in his image all people have inherent worth bestowed by their Creator. Therefore, you are your brother's keeper.

The world would soon forget the names and lives of the 23 men on trial that day. However, answers to the deeper questions that emerged from the trial are eternally important, because they affirm the relationship between God and humankind and define humankind's God-given responsibility to one another. Today almost 75 years removed from Nuremberg, we can clearly see how critically important this trial was to the preservation of Western civilization, but in real time, in the hot crucible of war, it was uncertain that this day of reckoning and justice in Nuremberg would ever happen. In fact, most in the West believed, the Nazi evil would prevail, because the war was being lost. In those desperate hours, presidents, prime ministers, and kings prayed pastoral prayers.

* * *

Washington, DC, two years and six months before the opening of the Nuremberg Trials

On the evening of June 6, 1944, Americans switched on their radios and heard the familiar voice of President Franklin D. Roosevelt. Early in his presidency during the darkest days of the Great Depression, the president's advisors discovered that he had a gift of being able to personally connect with Americans through radio. It was like he was in their living rooms speaking directly to them, and his broadcasts came to be called "Fireside Chats." On this night, the president had news that was encouraging and frightening at the same time.

American, British, and Canadian forces with the assistance of the French resistance were invading Normandy, France. The D-Day invasion was underway. The evening before, President Roosevelt had announced that Rome had been liberated from Nazi control. Tonight's message, however, wasn't an announcement of a victory, but an alert that a great battle had begun. For one side or the other, this battle would be decisive. The wealth of nations spent on planes, ships, bombs, and all the instruments of war, and the treasure of nations – their youth – were being hurled onto the beaches of Normandy. The outcome of this great battle was entirely uncertain, because the enemy's fortifications were sunk deep into the Norman cliffs, and these were manned by a determined German foe.

An ocean away from the battlefield, Americans were anxious. How would this great battle go? Would their sons come home? What would the world be like after all this was over? With the scent of fear in the air, President Roosevelt pulled the microphone closer and to the nation said, "And so, in this poignant hour, I ask you to join with me in prayer."

Almighty God,

Our sons, pride of our nation, this day have set upon a mighty endeavor, a struggle to preserve our Republic, our religion, and our civilization, and to set free a suffering humanity.

Lead them straight and true; give strength to their arms, stoutness to their hearts, steadfastness in their faith.

They will need Thy blessings. Their road will be long and hard. For the enemy is strong. He may hurl back our forces. Success may not come with rushing speed, but we shall return again and again; and we know that by Thy grace, and by the righteousness of our cause, our sons will triumph.

They will be sore tried, by night and by day, without rest – until the victory is won. The darkness will be rent by noise and flame. Men's souls will be shaken with the violences of war.

For these men are lately drawn from the ways of peace. They fight not for the lust of conquest. They fight to end conquest. They fight to liberate. They fight to let justice arise, and tolerance and goodwill among all Thy people. They yearn but for the end of battle, for their return to the haven of home.

Some will never return. Embrace these, Father, and receive them, Thy heroic servants, into Thy kingdom.

And for us at home – fathers, mothers, children, wives, sisters, and brothers of brave men overseas, whose thoughts and prayers are ever with them – help us, Almighty God, to rededicate ourselves in renewed faith in Thee in this hour of great sacrifice.

Many people have urged that I call the nation into a single day of special prayer. But because the road is long and the desire is great, I ask that our people devote themselves in a continuance of prayer. As we rise to each new day, and again when each day is spent, let words of prayer be on our lips, invoking Thy help to our efforts.

Give us strength, too – strength in our daily tasks, to redouble the contributions we make in the physical and the material support of our armed forces.

And let our hearts be stout, to wait out the long travail, to bear sorrows that may come, to impart our courage unto our sons wheresoever they may be.

And, O Lord, give us faith. Give us faith in Thee; faith in our sons; faith in each other; faith in our united crusade. Let not the keenness of our spirit ever be dulled. Let not the impacts of temporary events, of temporal matters of but fleeting moment – let not these deter us in our unconquerable purpose.

With Thy blessing, we shall prevail over the unholy forces of our enemy. Help us to conquer the apostles of greed and racial arrogances. Lead us to the saving of our country, and with our sister nations into a world unity that will spell a sure peace – a peace invulnerable to the schemings of unworthy men. And a peace that will let all of men live in freedom, reaping the just rewards of their honest toil.

Thy will be done, Almighty God.

Amen.

President Roosevelt did not live to see the "apostles of greed and racial arrogance" stand trial in Nuremberg. He died in Warm Springs, Georgia on April 12, 1945, more than a year before the trial took place. When he offered his pastoral prayer, no one knew the future or the providence that God had determined for our lives or for nations. So, we prayed, and on this early summer evening of 1944, the president asked Americans to pray continually. He said, "I ask that our people devote themselves in a continuance of prayer. As we rise to each new day, and again when each day is spent, let words of prayer be on our lips, invoking Thy help to our efforts."

Like King Solomon, who three thousand years before him, Roosevelt humbled himself before Almighty God. Hours earlier, the president's command had launched the largest invasion the world had ever witnessed. More military power was assembled in the English Channel off the coast of France than all previous armies and navies combined. Yet such power and might that moved by his mere words offered little comfort to the president, because it is Almighty God, who is sovereign and it is he who raises nations up and casts them down. Roosevelt and Solomon knew the limits of their power, and therefore, both leaders prayed the same prayer, "Hear from heaven and act." Knowing that their petitions may or may not be granted, the prayers end with a statement of faith, "Thy will be done, Almighty God. Amen."

This D-Day prayer wasn't the first pastoral prayer given by Roosevelt. Years earlier, we find him again praying at a desperate time.

* * *

Washington, DC, four years before the opening of the Nuremberg Trials

A cold gloom gripped the world on Sunday, January 1, 1942. There would be no raucous celebrations this New Year's Day in America. This first day of the new year was dedicated as a National Day of Prayer, and at this moment, prayer to an Almighty, Sovereign and Just God seemed the only hope for America. Only a few weeks earlier, Imperial Japan attacked the US Navy's Pacific Fleet anchored in Pearl Harbor, Hawaii. Over 2,400 sailors and Marines were dead and over a thousand more lay wounded. Ships that weren't resting on the bottom of the harbor were smothering wrecks. But, this was only part of the bad news.

Europe was experiencing one of its coldest winters on record, and the German army was at the gates of Stalingrad. If Russia fell to the Nazis, then only Great Britain remained to oppose Germany and Italy, the Axis powers in Europe. In this winter of desperation, Prime Minister Winston Churchill secretly crossed the Atlantic to meet with President Roosevelt. The task ahead was daunting, and planning and strategizing for how the two nations might begin to turn the tide of war took the bulk of their time together, but prayer was a priority too for it was the key to ultimate victory.

On this New Year's Day, the president and prime minister left the White House to attend worship services at Christ

Church in Alexandria, Virginia. Just a short carriage ride from Mount Vernon, this was George Washington's church, and his family's pew remains in the church today. On this Sunday morning, however, America's first Commander in Chief would quickly recognize the sights and sounds of war. Armed soldiers ringed the church's perimeter, and Secret Service roamed the church's grounds.

Soon, the president's motorcade appeared and quickly pulled to a stop near the church doors. Roosevelt and Churchill emerged, removed their hats, and entered. Once seated in Washington's pew, the Rev. Edward Randolph Welles began the worship service. In both, the sermon and pastoral prayer, the reverend asked the Lord Almighty to hear and act on three petitions. He asked that God would give strength to the nation in the coming conflict, that justice and peace would prevail, and that Christ would forgive the nation's sins. These petitions were similar to those of King Solomon, because the needs of nations and those who lead them in righteous endeavors are timeless.

For Churchill and Great Britain, this worship service offered great hope. Great Britain had struggled alone for almost two years. America, their friend and closest ally, was now in the presence of God committed to winning the war, and Churchill needed all the help he could get, because he knew that only prayer had saved the British army two years earlier.

* * *

London, five years and seven months before the opening of the Nuremberg Trials

In May 1940, the British army was in full retreat. The German army had the upper hand and was rapidly pushing the Brits across France and into the English Channel. With no place left to run, the British army was trapped near the town of Dunkirk. The sea was behind them and the German army in front, encircling them. Overhead, the Luftwaffe pounded the British positions. Surrender or certain annihilation seemed the only two options. Either way, the war seemed lost before it had hardily begun.

On May 23, Churchill met with King George VI and briefed His Majesty on the dismal situation. Churchill could offer no reasonable way of avoiding a massive defeat, but King George thought otherwise; he would call the nation to prayer. The next day, the king addressed the nation saying, "Let us with one heart and soul, humbly but confidently, commit our cause to God and ask his aid, that we may valiantly defend the right as it is given to us to see it." The national day of prayer was set for Sunday, May 26.

On that day, churches across Great Britain were filled. The Archbishop of Canterbury lead the service in Westminster Abbey, where he called on God to protect the British army. What happened over the next ten days is called the Miracle at Dunkirk. Hundreds of private boats large and small crossed the channel to rescue the troops and bring them home. Making this crossing possible was the most improbable weather. The channel was said never to have been calmer, the boats – most of which weren't built for channel crossing – had smooth sailing. On land it was a different story. Clouds and turbulence set in, grounding the Luftwaffe. The German planes were unable to fly, and the delay was just long enough to allow the escape. The army was saved to fight another day. Truly, it was a miracle. God in heaven heard and acted.

* * *

This backwards march in time from Nuremberg to Dunkirk reveals much about the West and prayer. For the West, it poignantly illustrates that once we were a people bound together in prayer and bound to Almighty God as one. Prayer was the holy cord tying us one to another. Even the powerful unashamedly bowed in prayer, because they knew their nations were in God's hands and subject to his providence. Therefore, prayer was not an afterthought, but an intentional part of everyday life. Through prayer, we had a refuge, a retreat, a resting place prepared by God. Whether or not God would grant the United States and Great Britain's prayers for victory in World War II was entirely unknown during the conflict. Still, Roosevelt, Churchill, and King George VI placed their petitions before God on behalf of their nations.

Through this act of faith and trust in God, the first benefit of prayer is revealed, hope. Prayer strengthens hope, and gives courage when fear seeks to overtake us. These benefits of prayer are felt, because our hope and courage are founded on who we know God to be. We know him through Jesus Christ, who has promised never to abandon us. Therefore, even when our petitions are denied, and things don't work out the way we want, we trust in God's sovereign purpose in our lives, and take comfort that no matter the circumstances, including death, Christ is with us. He knows our names, and we will rest with him in eternity. Now, that we know the nature of pastoral prayer, we have arrived at our final stop this backward journey through the war years. It is a place of unanswered prayers.

* * *

Normandy, France, 74 years after the opening of the Nuremberg Trials

High on a cliff in Normandy near Colleville-sur-Mer the wind off the English Channel blows briskly over 172 acres of manicured landscape. Daily, visitors stroll the grounds never hurrying and barely speaking above a whisper. Only the rustle of the wind and the quiet chimes of the clock tower disturbs the peace. Below the cliff, where land meets sea, is a brown sandy beach that Americans know as "Omaha." The cliff above is the final resting place of 9,387 young Americans, who lost their lives in the D-Day invasion in 1944. It's important to know just how young they were. Many were teenagers, not yet 20 years old.

The centerpiece of this American Cemetery is a striking sculpture entitled "The Spirit of American Youth Rising Above the Waves." It depicts a fit and muscular young man with one arm outstretched toward heaven and head tilted to the clouds. In this pose, he is lifted and rescued from turbulent waters. It is a reverent and poignant tribute to those who sacrificed their young lives.

Their prayers, and the prayers of a nation, for survival on Omaha Beach went unanswered. The horror of their final minutes of life on the beach is now the tranquility of their final resting place on the cliff, which is a metaphor for all of life and all prayers. Christ never abandons those who believe in him. Never! We will be with him in eternity. God does not forsake his people. Because of this promise, pastoral prayers through the thousands of years that they been offered conclude with similar words. King Solomon said, "Praise be to the Lord, who has given rest to his people... just as he promised." Three thousand years later, President Roosevelt said, "Thy will be done, Almighty God. Amen." And, amen.

Chapter 7: Anthem

Below is a passage from Psalm 57. It was composed and sung by David, as an anthem to celebrate deliverance from his enemy, King Saul. To Saul, David was a usurper to his throne, and Saul was intent on killing this young upstart. With Saul hot on his trail, David hid in a cave. The imagery employed in the psalm is a night of danger that is followed by a morning of deliverance and salvation. The night of danger and despair is poetically told in the first few verses. In the latter verses, dawn arrives and with it deliverance. In verse 8, David shouts with joy, "I will awaken the dawn," and he then concludes the psalm with praise to God. Hear now David's ancient yet timeless anthem.

They spread a net for my feet—
I was bowed down in distress.
They dug a pit in my path—
but they have fallen into it themselves.
7 *My heart, O God, is steadfast,*
my heart is steadfast;
I will sing and make music.
8 *Awake, my soul!*
Awake, harp and lyre!
I will awaken the dawn.
9 *I will praise you, Lord, among the nations;*
I will sing of you among the peoples.
10 *For great is your love, reaching to the heavens;*
your faithfulness reaches to the skies.
11 *Be exalted, O God, above the heavens;*
let your glory be over all the earth.
(Psalm 57:6-11)

Anthems sing of life and hope! When the world says "Be afraid," anthems sing of courage. When everyone says, "It's over; give-up," anthems sing of perseverance. When all seems lost, anthems rejoice in unexpected rescue. In gratitude for being granted courage, perseverance, and rescue, anthems are joyfully sung, because your exuberance and enthusiasm cannot be contained or constrained. This is the essence of an anthem, and the third stanza of America's National Anthem convincingly illustrates this definition:

And the rockets' red glare,
The bombs bursting in air,
Gave proof through the night
That our flag was still there.

In the darkness, the battle raged and certainly was being lost. But, have courage, and persevere. Dawn awaits, and "Our flag was still there."

In the section below, you will meet Arthur Stace, whose life was an anthem. There was the first half of his life, when he was an absolute wreck. But, Christ rescued him and gave him a mission for the second half of life. The 21st Century opened with a special message from God that was delivered to the world by Arthur Stace. Stace's God-given message was a single word, and for the West, this word is an anthem. Your long night of moral and spiritual darkness will come to an end. Remain steadfast! God is faithful. His salvation and deliverance is near. A new dawn will come. Now, let's meet Arthur Stace and hear his miraculous story.

* * *

From 1st Century Jerusalem to Sydney, Australia, New Year's Eve 1999

God's message of deliverance and hope was flashed to the world at precisely 12:24 AM, January 1, 2000. The new year – indeed the new century and the new millennium – were only 24 minutes old. When we think of messages from God, a scowling, bearded prophet covered in desert dust with staff in hand likely comes to mind. But, this New Year's message wasn't about judgment or the wrath of God. It was an anthem: deliverance is on the way, remain steadfast, and joy awaits. Therefore, the lead up to this message, or more specifically, the introduction of it needed to match the message by being courageous, joyful, and spectacular. And, it was! Hollywood and Disney would struggle to match the fanfare and showmanship that happened that night in Sydney Harbor. Never was the harbor more exciting or beautiful. With this New Year's Eve celebration, Sydney, due to her proximity to the International Dateline where each new day begins, welcomed the world to the new millennium. It was the perfect setting for God's message of hope.

The BBC estimated that a million Sydneysiders – that's what the citizens call themselves – crowded the harbor's shore and more than six thousand pleasure boats jammed the harbor's water, all vying for the best view of the iconic Opera House and Harbor Bridge. They had partied for hours and now the midnight moment had arrived. Lights surrounding the harbor magically extinguished. Suddenly, air sirens pieced the night air. The PA system boomed! ***Ignition sequence start. 12-11-10-9-8-7-6-5-4-3-2-1! Happy New Year!***

Ignition indeed! Fireworks rocked the city and filled the night sky with colorful brilliance. The new millennium was underway. As smoke from the initial blast of pyrotechnics cleared, revelers saw a giant smiley face illuminated in white lights staring back at them from the side of the Harbor Bridge. This new era was off to a whimsical, joyful start.

Over the next 23 minutes, with music, fanfare, and laser lights playing off the Opera House and Harbor Bridge, the celebration moved toward its dramatic climax. First was the final round of fireworks that surpassed anything seen before. Zooming upwards to 3,000 feet in the air, rockets exploded, raining their colorful payload on the city below. Fireworks from underneath the bridge ignited, sending white sparklers cascading like a waterfall into the dark harbor waters below. The giant smiley face switched off and as the few surviving embers from the last rocket drifted downward, the smoke parted, revealing a new illumination on the bridge. It was a single word: *Eternity*.

A million Sydneysiders – and hundreds of millions of people worldwide sitting at home in front of their TVs – watched in silence as a gentle breeze pushed away wispy lingering smoke. In the near darkness of the clear night sky, the word seemed to float above the harbor water, pushing back the darkness. The brilliance of the light touched the eye, but it was the magnitude of the message that touched the heart. The message is this: there is hope and abundant life. *Eternity* – the dwelling place of God – is where the message originated, and where God is there is hope and life. Do not despair. Do not give up hope. There is more to life than you can possibly imagine. Death itself has been conquered and lies defeated in the doorway of Christ's empty tomb. This is the power of *Eternity*, and now it was written on the side of a bridge for all the modern world to see. It was a sign and message from God that was an anthem – a new dawn awaits!

God communicates with we creatures who bear his image in many ways – through the beauty of his Creation, in the contentment of a newborn at mother's breast, through meals with family and friends, in the quietness of prayer, in comfort during suffering, in the joy of worship, and by mediation on scripture to name a few. Signs, however, are a primary way God communicates specific information. Noah, after the flood, saw the rainbow in the sky as God's sign of peace. Moses in the desert spied the burning bush and scripture tells us that "he turned aside" from his work of tending his father-in-law's flock to investigate this sign. In doing so, he heard the voice of God. Belshazzar, the King of Babylon, saw the hand of God writing on the palace wall, and of course, all the miracles of Jesus were signs and messages to humankind. To place the word *Eternity* on the Sydney Harbor Bridge in this category may seem like hyperbole, but the decades of events leading up to that New Year's celebration were nothing short of miraculous! The story begins with an obscure, illiterate alcoholic, who was born into a hard-scrabble life of late 19th Century Australia.

Arthur Malcolm Stace was born in 1885 in a western suburb of Sydney.[15] His childhood and early adult years offered no presage that one day he might deliver to the world a message from God. His mother and father were alcoholics and he was raised in abject poverty. As a young child, he stole milk and bread, and foraged neighbors' garbage for scraps of food. He rarely attended school and by age 12, he was working in a coal mine. What today is known as child protection services stepped in and assumed legal guardianship, but his circumstances showed little improvement. In his teen years, he became an alcoholic and petty criminal, serving as a look-out for robbers and prostitutes. The prostitutes were sadly his sisters.

At age 32, he enlisted to fight in World War I, and in 1919 he was medically discharged. For the next dozen years, he knocked about Sydney as a drunk, working odd jobs while daily succumbing to the rages of alcoholism and poverty. Then, miraculously on the night of August 3, 1930, he experienced the call of the Eternal God. In an instant, his life changed. He stopped drinking, and as his mind sobered, he became intrigued with the idea of eternity, which was the first inkling of his life's mission.

Two years later, on November 14, 1932, he was inspired by the evangelistic preaching of John G. Ridley, who drew his sermon from Isaiah 57:15:

For thus says the One who is high and lifted up,
who inhabits eternity, whose name is Holy:
"I dwell in the high and holy place,
and also with him who is of a contrite and lowly spirit,
to revive the spirit of the lowly,
and to revive the heart of the contrite."

This scripture sank deep into Arthur's contrite and lowly spirit. The Lord God, who created all things and dwells in eternity, revived Arthur's heart and gave him a new spirit. This miraculous turn of events needed to be joyfully expressed and shared. With this thought in mind, his mission in life became clear. Leaving his house each morning around 5 AM with a bit of chalk in his pocket, Arthur wrote *Eternity* throughout downtown Sydney. On walls, on sidewalks, on benches, at bus and train stations, on doorsills – anywhere there was space – he legibly wrote *Eternity* in a calligraphy script called copperplate. Yet, he could barely write his own name. He said, "the word 'Eternity' came out smoothly, in a beautiful copperplate script. I couldn't understand it, and I still can't."

For 35 years from 1932 to 1967, he wrote the word an estimated half-million times, and became known as "Mr. Eternity." Of course, not everyone appreciated his graffiti, and he was apprehended by police about 24 times. Each time when questioned, he responded, "But I had permission from a higher source," and he was released. His mission completed, God took

Arthur to the place he wrote about so much. "Mr. Eternity" died of a stroke on July 30, 1967.

Over 30 years later, the committee responsible for Sydney's New Year's millennium celebration chose to end the event with Arthur's message. Later in 2000, Sydney hosted the Olympic Games, and *Eternity* once again was illuminated on the Harbor Bridge for all the world to see. Arthur, not only faithfully delivered God's message; his life was God's message. His life was an anthem. Like David's dark night of fear in the cave that was followed by a dawn of deliverance, Arthur's life was a story of contrasting halves. From the darkness, fear, and ravages of alcoholism, poverty, and crime, God freed him, giving him a new dawn of life. Arthur's life story is the essence of anthem. Don't give up! There is hope, because God hasn't given up on us.

Now that we know David and Arthur's stories and the anthem of their lives, what is our story? Do Western men and women live life as an anthem with the expectation that God, who dwells in eternity, will revive our spirits? The answer is no. We have no expectation that God even exists. To remedy our unbelief, each morning God sent Arthur Stace out his front door at 5 AM with a message that remarkably 30 years later city leaders in Sydney chose to broadcast to the world, not once, but twice! Now, it's up to us receive this message, comprehend it, and live it. To do these things, we now must peer into the dark shadows of our time and identify the nets spread for our feet and the pits dug into our paths. In the darkness of the cave, David knew that Saul had set traps and snares to catch and kill him. In the dark cave of drunkenness, Arthur knew that disease, danger, and poverty stalked him and one day would kill him. What stalks us? It is time, fear, and death.

These are the exact opposites of God's message delivered by Arthur. Eternity is timeless. It is the dwelling place of God, and where God is there is hope – the opposite of fear – and there is life – the opposite of death. Yet, we know that time, fear, and death have always stalked humanity. They are part of the human condition to which Christ Jesus is the answer. Therefore, the substantive question is, not what stalks us, but why are 21st Century Western men and women so fearful about everything, so willingly believe deadlines of pending doom, and so readily imagine death everywhere? The answer to this question is written in our daily lives.

Westerners fear everything! We fear that driving our cars, heating and cooling our homes, and cooking on a backyard grill will bring death to planet. This fear is eminent. It's not a far-off thing. We are constantly reminded that greenhouses gases and our use of fossil fuels will kill Earth in a dozen years. We even fear that cows farting in a pasture will kill the planet and us with it! We fear drinking water or soda from a plastic bottle. Surely, that raft of plastic floating in the Pacific Ocean grows by the day, and because we use plastic, we fear we are killing whales, dolphins, and sea turtles. We fear storms of every type. Snowstorms are no longer just a part of winter. They are epic and threatening. Tropical storms are now given names so they can more easily be feared. Hurricanes have always been named, but today they don't just come ashore and cause damage. Agnes, Camille, Katrina, and Matthew are menacing killers roaming the sea and waiting to pounce and hopelessly devour us. But, where will they strike? The experts – who are the modern equivalent of wizards and diviners – don't know for sure so we all should be very afraid. We fear disease. From cancer to incontinence, diseases are personified so that now it's not a disease, but a threating person that we must unite against and fight from a position of fear. Of course, the West really feared COVID-19. All Western economies shut down due to fears of that virus, and when a dispassionate history is written, the coronavirus will have turned out to be a season of influenza that was worse than some seasons, and not as bad as others. We fear what we eat. Is our food locally sourced? Is our coffee fair-trade? Is it immoral to eat meat? Shouldn't we be vegans? Our fear is not limited to what we eat, we fear simply eating, as witnessed by numerous eating disorders. These are acute fears, i.e., dread and anxiety of things with dire consequences that are not far off. This list could be much longer, but we need to move onto chronic fears, because these too make for a long list.

Westerners fear growing old. We fear commitment in relationships even while we have a great fear of loneliness. We fear having children, because parenting is a long-term commitment that will surely hinder our lifestyle, and when we do have children, we fear making mistakes in raising and educating them. From these fears, a whole industry of (mostly bad) parenting advice has arisen. Once grown, we fear that our children cannot support themselves, and fear they may move back home. We fear that our marriages, friendships, and family relationships will fail. We fear losing our jobs. We fear being called racist, and we fear that we will never escape the racist label, because now there is latent and systemic racism. We fear being anti-LGBTQ+, and politically incorrect. (Although these fears, rightfully belong in the acute category because people are cancelled and lose their livelihoods, reputations, friends, and even family.) We fear the future, and when told that Western suicide rates are rising, we wring our hands and fear that we are so fearful. This list of nagging chronic fears could go on, but we will end it here, because they are important points to make and conclusions to draw.

Bound up in all these fears is time and death. Notice how all these fears, whether acute or chronic, have a time value and doom associated with them. Earth will be destroyed in a dozen years. Timing is running out for the oceans – whales, dolphins, and sea turtles will soon be gone upsetting the ocean ecosphere with disastrous consequences. Fear of being a bad parent – they're only children for just so long! Fear of growing old camps at the intersection of time and death. I must drink only fair-trade coffee, because time is running out for farmers in the developing world. Let's not forget that the Amazon rainforest will be gone in a decade or so. For Westerners death is everywhere, including the womb, and the time in which abortions can be legally performed in Western nations has increased including all the way up to the moment of birth. Why is it that 21st Westerners are haunted by fear, deadlines, and doom everywhere and in everything?

Please! Can we just drink a cup of coffee without guilt and fear? No? Well, why not?

For the answer, we must go back to Psalm 57 and King Saul chasing David into a cave. In this situation we see the clash of two kingdoms – the kingdom of the world represented by Saul, and the kingdom of God represented by David. Remember that David's defining characteristic for leadership was that his heart desired the heart of God, and Saul had by his actions rejected God's kingdom and embraced the kingdom of the world.

These two kingdoms occupy the same physical reality and exist side-by-side at the same time, but they are populated by two very different people and produce divergent outcomes with the kingdom of the world producing fear and death and the kingdom of God giving hope and life. Efforts to define and identify the two kingdoms in 21st Century Western nations quickly becomes complicated and confusing, because when it comes to the kingdom of the world all the "isms" come in play: globalism, environmentalism, classism, sexism, racism, colonialism, Darwinism, Marxism, atheism, communism, consumerism, narcissism, pessimism, socialism, cynicism, barbarism, hedonism, nihilism, and even Satanism. Likewise, trying to describe the kingdom of God is fraught with difficulty. Attempting to explain the kingdom of God to haughty vain Westerners, who believe themselves to be educated gods yet lacking the most basic biblical knowledge, is like describing the beauty of a symphony to a person deaf since birth. Fortunately, there is a single measurable characteristic of the West that perfectly depicts both kingdoms, and this metric is quickly understood and not debatable. It is birthrate.

The birthrate among native-born indigenous Westerners is appalling low, because we fear commitment, fear responsibility, and especially fear that the joy of holy matrimony for the purpose of procreation could never surpass a life of libertine uncommitted sexual expression. Now, we are at the root of our fear. We have so debased and corrupted ourselves in all aspects of life that we cannot imagine a life in the kingdom of God. For Westerners we can only see the fear, deadlines, and doom of the kingdom of the world. We don't procreate, because the spirit of life and hope is so far from us that we cannot imagine selfless love for another person, and certainly cannot imagine the transcendent love of Our Savior. Our birthrate is in fact so low that, if left unchanged, some populations may eventually disappear.

In 2016, a very insightful writer for the Irish Times noted with alarm the West's declining birthrate and wrote: [16]

European civilisation is dying. It is dying in plain sight and almost nobody is talking about it. No, our civilisation is not succumbing to onslaught from an external foe. But we seem to be suffering from a pernicious anaemia of the spirit that drags us down from inside. There are many symptoms of this decline but the most deadly is that we are losing the will to breed. Birth rates in all 28 EU countries are now below replacement rates and all indigenous populations are in decline.

All the 21st Century "isms" that the kingdom of the world has put in the heart of Western men and women is the "pernicious anaemia of the spirit that drags us down from inside." This anemia of the spirt is why we are fearful, and why we see death everywhere in everything. It is because our civilization is dying. An aging society, like an aging person, grows hesitant, fearful, and less hopeful. The trend of declining birthrates has been underway for decades, and all Western nations have remedied it by increasing immigration of non-Western people. Germany, France, the United States, Great Britain, and indeed all Western nations need young people, who can work and produce. But, immigration without assimilation creates a whole new set of tensions and fears. As the anemia of our spirit deepens, we become more aware of our untenable moral, spiritual, and life situation. It's like we are living in the ninth plague that God visited upon pharaoh and ancient Egypt. Exodus 10:22 says the ninth plague was "a darkness that can be felt." The darkness in the West has been growing for a very long time, and now we feel it. It is the handiwork of the kingdom of the world.

In opposition to the kingdom of the world is the kingdom of God and for God's kingdom, birthrate is a telling metric that is written into Creation itself. Genesis 1:28 says:

And God blessed them [Adam and Eve], *and God said unto them, Be fruitful, and multiply, and replenish the earth, and subdue it.*

Westerners once overwhelmingly believed the verse and from believing it ensued a great civilization, populated by children and families, farmers and doers, thinkers and artists, dreamers and explorers, who welcomed the kingdom of God. Sadly today, increasingly few of us believe the verse and would not welcome the kingdom of God. This is the darkness of the ninth plague that we feel. This is why we fear everything and see death everywhere. Just as Saul's kingdom of the world chased David's kingdom of God into a dark cave, Christians have been chased into a darkness and are hiding. But wait, this is only the first half of our anthem – the half that we are now living. The second half awaits.

It will begin like each new day begins with dawn pushing back the darkness to an awakening world. It is by God's providence that each new day begins, and likewise, the great moral and spiritual awakening of the West will begin when the Holy Spirit pushes back the darkness of our fear. People will search for Christ Jesus and want to know him. Like David emerging from his cave at dawn, Christians will come out of hiding. People, who have lived for so long in the darkness that can be felt will ask, "Who are you?" We will say, "We are Christians," and they will reply, "I've been praying to God that you would come." As these words sink into our souls, we will think back to our seemingly endless night in the cave and wonder why did we ever doubt? In the darkness, God placed a bit of chalk in the hand of a most unlikely man and planted a single word in his heart, and because of Arthur Stace's faithfulness God wrote *Eternity* on the side of a bridge and illuminated it for all the world to see. At that moment, we will know that our anthem is complete. We will join with David and shout:

8 Awake, my soul!
Awake, harp and lyre!
I will awaken the dawn.
9 I will praise you, Lord, among the nations;
I will sing of you among the peoples.

Chapter 8: Offertory

41 And Jesus sat over against the treasury, and beheld how the people cast money into the treasury: and many that were rich cast in much. 42 And there came a certain poor widow, and she threw in two mites, which make a farthing. 43 And he called unto him his disciples, and saith unto them, Verily I say unto you, That this poor widow hath cast more in, than all they which have cast into the treasury. (Mark 12:41-43 KJV)

This well know passage from the King James Version gave rise to the expression "the widow's mite." Past generations, who were more biblically literate, were readily familiar with the expression. Today it's still heard, but less frequently. Those earlier generations knew the widow's mite meant someone had given their all, had made a huge sacrifice. Certainly, this passage from Mark is about sacrificial giving, but it's also about giving when the gift and giver are known only to God. Anonymity is an aspect of this encounter in the Temple. Note that Jesus did not call the widow over, ask her name, introduce her to his disciples, and then praise her for her gift. She remained anonymous, and likely did not even know that Jesus was observing her. The "two mites, which make a farthing" were a sacrificial gift from a selfless giver, who only desired recognition from God in heaven.

Jesus taught that anonymity is an important part of giving. In Matthew, he said:

3 But when you give to the needy, do not let your left hand know what your right hand is doing, 4 so that your giving may be in secret. Then your Father, who sees what is done in secret, will reward you. (Matthew 6:3-4)

Of course, your one hand knows what the other hand is doing, but Jesus was using hyperbole to illustrate the importance of the gift and giver being known only to God. Perhaps, the reason Jesus did not call the widow over and acknowledge her in front of his disciples is because he knew that being known to God was sufficient for her. Therefore, was she really anonymous? No, she was known to her Creator, and the fact that those in the Temple did not even notice her was inconsequential. She was known to God, and that's all that mattered. What is the character and heart of a person, whose desire to be known to God is greater than the desire to be known to others?

The widow possessed the rarest of character traits. She had equal portions of dignity and humility. Dignity arises from the knowledge that you are a unique individual, who is created in the image of the Lord God. Humility comes from knowing that the Lord God created everyone else in his image too. To make such a character assessment based on three short verses of scripture seems like a stretch. The fact is that other than being a widow, we know nothing at all about this woman, but there are important clues. The gospel writer, Mark, tells us that Jesus was observing "how the people cast their money into the treasury," and that the "rich cast in much." Therefore, Jesus was watching both the "how" and the "how much" of giving. Something about how this widow gave her two mites caught Jesus' attention. He sensed something in her character and attitude, and we too make similar judgments about people. Based on nothing more than how a person enters a room, we'll assume a person is strong and assertive, and say, "He's an alpha male." Or in the opposite, we might say, "That person is a shrinking violet." If we are capable of such snap judgments, which experience teaches are at least sometimes correct, then certainly Jesus is capable of even a deeper assessment of a person's character.

Because Jesus singled this woman out as noteworthy for praise tells us that her character was rare. Humility is the most uncommon of virtues. In fact, it's so uncommon and misunderstood that Westerner's today don't recognize humility when we see it. When we think of a humble person, doormat is likely the first word that pops into our minds. We think of them as weak, passive, and unwilling to assert themselves. For Westerners, humility does not equate to strength of character and virtue yet the humble person possesses these. And, we're equally confused by dignity. A decade or so ago, we confused achievement, success, and status with dignity. We thought that because a person had a university degree, success in business or the professions, and achieved some degree of wealth then they were dignified. But, that's status, not dignity. Dignity is displayed by a person who knows that their inherent self-worth comes from God, and not from degrees, success, or wealth. This is the dignity that Jesus saw in the widow. Sadly today, dignity – even the faux dignity that comes from social status – has nearly vanished. Today, the most undignified, crude, and obscene behavior is celebrated! If a dignified, humble, giving, and genuine person was rare during Jesus' time on earth, how are we to ever to find a modern-day version of the widow; someone of dignity and humility who gave their all, who gave their two mites?

First, we must look for someone who made a sacrificial gift; someone who had nothing to give except one thing, and then at great cost to themselves, they freely gave that gift to another. We find such a person – not a widow, but a young single woman – in rural Alabama near the end of the 19th Century. Her gift, when understood within the context of her poverty, deprivation, and physical challenges, was so extraordinary that her life has been the subject of books, movies and a Broadway play. Before we journey back more than one hundred years to the red clay hills of north Alabama to meet this woman, we must learn her life story. To hear that story, we will travel to rural Massachusetts in the 1860's. Let's go there now.

* * *

From 1st Century Jerusalem to Feeding Hills, Massachusetts, 1866.

She was born on April 14, 1866, and her parents, Thomas and Alice, gave her the name Johanna, but they always called her Ann or Annie. Ann, perhaps like the widow that Jesus spotted in the Temple, was born into generational poverty. Thomas and Alice were among the million or so poor, who left Ireland for America during the "An Gorta Mór." In Irish this means "The Great Hunger," and today it's better known as the Potato Famine. The ones who left were the lucky ones. Among those who stayed more than a million men, women, and children died of starvation, and it all began with a fungus that caused potatoes, the main food crop of the poor, to rot in the ground. This famine was of biblical proportions, lasting from 1845 to 1852. It was hunger that brought Thomas and Alice, and a million other Irish to America. Surely, a better life awaited in central Massachusetts, and in Feeding Hills, the couple started to rebuild their lives and began a family. Ann was the oldest, and soon she had a younger brother, James who was called Jimmie, and a sister, Mary. Things were looking up for a while, but then, like Job's family in the Bible, things went terribly wrong!

At age five, Ann suffered a series of painful eye infections known as trachoma. With no antibiotics, she suffered multiple infections that over time scared her eyes so badly she was nearly blind. When Ann was eight, her mother, Alice, died of tuberculosis, leaving Thomas with three children to raise, one of whom could barely see. For two years, he struggled to keep his family together and feed them, but eventually he was overwhelmed. The youngest, Mary, was sent to live with an aunt. Ann and Jimmie were sent to a crowded, squalid almshouse in Tewksbury, Massachusetts. Jimmie, who was already weakened by a hip condition, did not last long. Four months after arriving, he, like his mother, died of TB. Ann was now all alone, and living in a place of filth and disease. Jimmie had been her eyes. How would she manage? And, she was only ten years old. Surely, the widow in the Temple had an easier life! But, there was more yet to come for Ann to endure. In the mid-1870's medical practices were unsanitary, crude, and painful. Under these conditions, Ann was subjected to two eye surgeries, both of which were unsuccessful.

Conditions were so awful at the Tewksbury almshouse that the Board of State Charities initiated an investigation. Two years after the investigation, Ann was sent to a Catholic hospital in Lowell, where she endured a third unsuccessful eye operation. Fortunately, she remained at the hospital for several months, helping the nuns where she could. But, then a fourth operation was attempted and it yielded the same result – no improvement. Now twelve, she was sent back to Tewksbury. She could have been housed in the infirmary with the ill and insane, but instead she received a small act of mercy and was sent to the ward for single mothers and unmarried pregnant women. There she remained for three years until Franklin Benjamin Sanborn visited the almshouse.

Sanborn was the State Inspector of Charities, but more importantly, he was the founder of the Perkins School for the Blind in Boston. During his visit to Tewksbury, Ann begged him to allow her to attend Perkins. Ann wasn't a good candidate. She was barely – if all – educated. Her life had been spent in dreadful institutions that dehumanize and beat down a person's spirt. As a result, her social skills were crude and rough at best. At age 14, could this blind girl be taught to read and write? Could she learn life skills that would allow a young woman to live in a big city like Boston? It seemed doubtful yet Sanborn accepted her and she entered Perkins in 1880.

Sanborn's instinct to take a chance on Ann was good. While she got off to a rough start, she was soon making rapid progress, and she made a friend, Laura Bridgman. Laura was both blind and deaf, and in order to communicate with her, Ann learned the manual alphabet, which is a form of fingerspelling. Sitting together, they spelled words into each other's hand and this is perhaps the first hint of Ann's giving spirit. She took the time to learn a skill simply to be a friend. Also, while at Perkins, Ann underwent more eye surgeries, but these were successful and her eyesight improved. In 1886 at age 20, she graduated as valedictorian of her class, and in her speech to the class she said:

Fellow-graduates: Duty bids us go forth into active life. Let us go cheerfully, hopefully, and earnestly, and set ourselves to find our especial part. When we have found it, willingly and faithfully perform it; for every obstacle we overcome, every success we achieve tends to bring man closer to God and make life more as He would have it.[17]

These words offer a window into Ann's heart. Events of life conspired against her as a child, throwing every possible challenge, hardship, and deprivation at her. She spent most of her childhood institutionalized, and she endured multiple crude eye operations. Worse, she went through all this alone. Or was she? Ann said, "Let us go cheerfully, hopefully, and earnestly..." These are remarkable words. Why was she not bitter and angry that God had allowed such terrible things to happen to her, her mother, brother, and father, and in fact all the people of Ireland? When asked about suffering, theologians talk about God's sovereign will, meaning that nothing happens unless it is the will of the Father. (Matthew 10:29) But, then you are left with the numb and frightening feeling that God would bring such suffering to a young child like Ann. So, theologians point to God's permissive will, meaning that since the fall of man in Eden, evil is in the world and in God's divine purpose bad things happen even to innocent children, i.e., it's not God's will but he permits it. (Romans 1:21-23) This age-old dilemma of why bad things happen to good people viewed through the theological lens of God's sovereign and permissive wills leaves us with two things. First, we clearly see why people generally don't care for theology, and second, we clearly see the limit of our human understanding, leaving us in exactly the place where God wants us. We are left with a single choice: to live by faith or not.

Through Ann's own cheerful and hopeful words, we see her choice. She had faith, and God rewarded her with an unwavering conviction that human dignity comes only from Our Creator. It is our birthright and nothing – not blindness, not death, not the Tewksbury almshouse – could take that away from Ann. Yet, we ourselves can choose to throw away this birthright. Sadly, most people do. The story of people throwing it away occurs in the Old and New Testaments. It is the story of Esau (Genesis 25:32) and the Prodigal Son. (Luke 15:12)

Throwing away the dignity of being created in the image of God is certainly the story of this generation of Westerners, and in doing so, we have exchanged the hope and joy that comes from heaven for the depression and disappointment of this world. The result is that far too many Westerners live with a loneliness of the soul that Ann, based upon her graduation speech, never experienced even in the darkest days at Tewksbury. God's presence in Ann's soul filled her whole being, and perhaps that is what Sanborn saw in her – a spirit of dignity that he wanted at Perkins School for the Blind. Dignity, however, was only one-half of the remarkable character that both Ann and the widow in the Bible possessed. Humility was the other half. Soon after graduation, Ann's humility was demonstrated and her precious gift – her two mites which make a farthing – was made.

A few short months after graduation, a letter from the father of a seven-year old girl in Alabama arrived at Perkins. Sentence by sentence, the father's desperation and heartfelt concern for his daughter were expressed. At birth, she was a normal healthy baby, but before the age of two, she came down with an unknown and terrible illness that the doctors' described as "an acute congestion of the stomach and the brain." Perhaps, it was rubella, scarlet fever, a flu, or something else. Whatever the disease, it left his little girl blind and deaf, and now she was seven years old. For five years that developmentally are crucial and can never be replaced, the child was locked away in a dark and soundless world. Could the school send a teacher to help his little girl? This was the father's earnest plea.[18]

Michael Anagnos, the director of the Perkins School, knew the one person best suited and most capable of helping the child was Ann. She was their top student and more importantly, because of her friendship with Laura, Ann was proficient at fingerspelling and familiar with the unique challenges of dual disabilities. But, would she take the job? Would she, having just graduated and beginning her adult life in Boston, be willing to travel to the South? It was 1886, and memory of the Civil War was still raw and fresh. Ann laid all these concerns aside. There was a child alone and locked away from the world as surely as she had been locked away in the Tewksbury almshouse. Not knowing the circumstances that awaited her and uncertain that she could help this little girl, Ann accepted the position and arrived in northern Alabama in 1887.

To say that Ann's new job in the Deep South got off to a bad start is an understatement. She argued with the family about the Civil War, and she chastised them for being former slave owners. She did, however, establish a bond with the little girl, but progress was slow. Daily, Ann finger spelled words into the child's palm, but making the connection that finger movements in the hand symbolized words, and those words represented objects in the environment would require a cognitive leap – an "Aha!" moment.

In the movie that was made about Ann's life, the "Aha!" moment came when Ann held the little girl's hand under running water while finger spelling "water." The connection was made, and the child's prison door opened. Perhaps, the connection is now made for you too. The child was Helen Keller and the teacher was Ann Sullivan. The title of the movie about Ann's life is "The Miracle Worker." It was originally made for TV and aired in 1957. The story, however, was so compelling, it was made into a feature length film starring Anne Bancroft as Ann, and Patty Duke as Helen. The movie premiered in theaters in 1962.

At Ann's urging, Helen's parents enrolled her in the Perkins School. Her progress was phenomenal, and Helen became a public symbol for the school, and an example of what people with disabilities can accomplish, if given a chance. After Perkins, Helen continued her education and graduated from Radcliffe College. Throughout all the years, Ann was there at Helen's side. Both women received numerous awards and honorary degrees for their achievements. In 1936 at age 70, Ann passed away as Helen held her hand, the same hand that had signed the word "water" and changed Helen's life, and in turn changed the lives of untold thousands of others coping with disabilities. Surely, Jesus' words regarding the widow, when he said, "this poor widow hath cast more in, than all they which have cast into the treasury," apply to Ann.

Ann had nothing –no family, no wealth, and no home. Yet what she had – her two mites – was finger spelling and a generous heart, and of these she gave freely. In her valedictory speech to the Perkins' graduates, Ann said that when we have found our calling, we should "willingly and faithfully perform it; for every obstacle we overcome, every success we achieve tends to bring man closer to God and make life more as He would have it." In these words, we see Ann's humility. What little she had, she offered back to God, not for personal gain, nor for fame, awards or accolades. All these were given to her, but she sought none of them.

In 1887, Ann boarded a train for Alabama, because a little girl, who was blind and deaf, needed her and the two mites that she possessed. We have seen Ann's dignity in refusing to be crushed by her life circumstances. She was created in the image of God. Now, we see her humility. Everyone else is created in His image too so she set about to "make life more as He would have it." She humbly gave her two mites to carry out her Maker's sovereign will.

In the soul of man, dignity and humility are like two strong and sturdy tree branches, growing from the trunk of faith. Over a lifetime, as this tree of life is fed by scripture and prayer, watered with tears of failure and heartbreaks, and pruned by the hand of successes and achievements that we know could only have been accomplished with the help of others what emerges is a character of beauty, strength, and grace. Something else happens too. All the other virtues, like nesting birds, make their homes in the shelter of the strong and protective limbs of dignity and humility. Justice, courage, prudence, hope, forbearance, mercy, charity, and love live in the boughs, secure in the knowledge that though the winds of life may push and sway them, the trunk of faith and limbs of dignity and humility will never fail.

Rare is the person of such strong character! So rare that Jesus pointed the widow out to his disciples for special recognition. And so rare that books, movies, and a Broadway play were made about Ann. But, those stories of Ann's life are now over 60 years old, and this tells us something very important about the people we have become.

What is the character to which we aspire? What are the virtues we wish to instill in our children? Yes, the widow and Ann's character were rare, but both in scripture and in the popular media of the 1950's and '60s, their character and lives were held up as exemplary, and worthy of imitation. But the same is not true today. And, perhaps the reason that Western men and women no longer aspire to a life of faith, dignity, humility, and virtue is because these are the things of the spirit. These are the things of our birthright that – like Esau and the Prodigal Son – we have throwaway. When society tells its citizens that you are not created in the image of God, but simply a mass of tissue, blood, and bones, then the light of the Spirit of God vanishes, leaving us in the spiritual darkness we live in today. But, for those of us who know that we are created in the image of God and that we are eternal creatures, who are saved by Christ, we have two mites. We have dignity and humility. These foundational virtues are our two mites, and we give them by living lives that illustrate them in our words and deeds.

This statement sounds so idealistic and pious, because frankly it is. But, is that a bad thing? No. A virtuous life of faith, dignity, and humility is what every person – but especially Christians – should aspire to yet we don't. Clawing us away from this noble aspiration is Western cynicism that daily seeks to crush any thoughts of God out of us. But, is our situation any worse than what Ann endured in Tewksbury almshouse, where daily the institution sought to crush her humanity? Of course not, and Ann's life has one final lesson to teach us. Living a life guided by faith, dignity, and humility doesn't mean you're perfect. Look at Ann from the point of view of the Keller family.

Mr. Keller with great effort, care, and expense – remember there was no internet in the 1880's – hired a specially trained tutor and governess for his daughter, and what did he get? A judgmental Yankee girl, who upon arrival argued about the Civil War, reprimanded them for being former slave owners, and at least at the start wasn't doing that great of job teaching his daughter. Ann wasn't perfect, and it's a safe bet that the widow in the Bible wasn't either. Yet, they both received recognition for living a life of faith, dignity, and humility, and in the end, they both freely gave their two mites. And, so can we. A tree does not reach maturity and its final shape over a single summer, but over a lifetime. Therefore, let our aspiration throughout life be to live by faith and in doing so gain dignity and humility.

As Jesus stood in the Temple, he watched how and how much people gave. Whatever two mites God has given us, let us give them freely through faith and with dignity, humility, and anonymity. That Jesus knows of our gift is all that matters. We don't know what heaven is like, but if the how and how much of our giving is like that of the widow, then perhaps, when we arrive at the heavenly gate, Jesus will call his disciples over and say, "Verily I say unto you, That this [person] hath cast more in, than all they which have cast into the treasury."

Chapter 9: Sermon, Proclamation of God's Word

So, faith comes from hearing, and hearing through the word of Christ. (Romans 10:17)

How odd! A typical first thought is that faith comes from seeing, as in: if only I could see Jesus, then I would believe. This thinking is bolstered by the apostles and the hundreds of others who saw the resurrected Christ and believed. But, if "seeing is believing" is the main source of faith, then the opportunity to believe was very short indeed and limited to those alive in the months following the resurrection. Not only would you have to be alive at that time in the 1st Century, but you would also have to live in or around Jerusalem to be able to see and believe. Therefore, hearing, perhaps through necessity, became the primary means of spreading faith in Jesus Christ, as the Savior of humankind. But, something else happens when we hear the gospel message spoken in a sermon, read from scripture, or shared by a friend. We hear another voice speaking to us. It is the voice of the Holy Spirit speaking to our hearts. A.W. Tozer, a 20th Century theologian, preacher, and writer described the experience as follows:

"When the Spirit illuminates the heart, then a part of the man sees which never saw before; a part of him knows which never knew before, and that with a kind of knowing which the most acute thinker cannot imitate. He knows now in a deep and authoritative way, and what he knows needs no reasoned proof. His experience of knowing is above reason, immediate, perfectly convincing and inwardly satisfying.[19]

Tozer's description of a heart awakened by faith reveals the deep mystery of the Holy Spirit. When we hear the gospel message, the Holy Spirit enlivens the word, illuminates the heart, and the result is an "experience of knowing" that is "immediate, perfectly convincing and inwardly satisfying." Such is the commanding authority of words empowered by the Spirit of God.

Deep in the Sinai Desert, Moses heard the words "I AM" spoken from the burning bush, and the Spirit of God in those two words launched the Exodus and the birth of the nation of Israel. Centuries later, the angel, Gabriel, spoke the words of God to Mary telling her, "Do not be afraid;" "the power of the Most High will overshadow you," and "the child to be born will be called holy – the Son of God." (Luke 1:30, 35) Those words initiated the greatest event in all of human history, as told in the four gospels, Matthew, Mark, Luke, and John. The core message of the gospels is this: Jesus Christ is resurrected; death itself has been conquered.

Each Sunday is a celebration of the resurrection, and when preachers proclaim the Word of God from the pulpit, they are proclaiming Christ's resurrection. For two thousand years, hearing this proclamation has changed lives and shaped every aspect of Western civilization. When we sit in the pew on Sunday morning to hear the proclamation of Christ's resurrection, we are taking our place in the great centuries old congregation of saints who came before us. Sadly, we live in a time when far too many preachers lack confidence in the power of hearing the gospel message, and as a result, their sermons are weak, insipid, ill-informed, rambling, boring, and the list of unflattering descriptors could go on. How unfortunate, because when the Word of God is proclaimed, the Spirit, as Tozer said, illuminates the heart. A new spirit – the Spirit of God – is born in the person and it all begins with hearing. Hearing spirit inspired words is powerful!

In the following story, the power of hearing to shape character, give hope where hope is lost, transform cowardice into courage, and bring about deliverance and salvation when neither seemed possible is illustrated through hearing spirit inspired mottos. When we speak a spirit inspired motto, our voice joins with voices, who spoke the same words in the past, and in a sense, we hear their voices in unison with ours. A third voice also joins in, and this voice arises, because the spirit of the words link us to a higher calling, something that is beyond ourselves, and therefore, the spirit of the motto speaks to our spirit. Perhaps, it is a tradition, an institution, a nation, a cause, or even Christ himself. Like instruments in an orchestra, these voices of the past, present, and higher calling uniquely blend even while maintaining their individuality, and in doing so, they speak powerfully to our souls. In the story below, we will learn how two spirit inspired mottos have changed lives and shaped our civilization.

* * *

From 1st Century Jerusalem to West Point, New York, May 12, 1962

"As I was leaving the hotel this morning, a doorman asked me, "Where are you bound for, General?" and when I replied, "West Point," he remarked, "Beautiful place, have you ever been there before?" With this humorous opening remark, General Douglas MacArthur began his speech to the Corps of Cadets at the United States Military Academy. Been there before indeed! He first stepped foot on campus at the end of the 19th Century and graduated as First Captain and with top honors in the class of 1903. In the 1920's, after seeing action in World War I, MacArthur returned to West Point to serve as the Academy's superintendent. Now, at age 82, the old general was back to receive the Sylvanus Thayer Award that is named in honor of the 18th Century colonel, who is credited as being the "Father of the Military Academy."

During his long military career, MacArthur received numerous awards and medals for bravery, including the Medal of Honor. The Thayer Award, however, is a medal recognizing not heroism or achievement, but character. It is a medal given annually to an individual, whose character exemplifies the Academy's motto of Duty, Honor, Country. Perhaps it was the emotion of returning to the place of his youth, perhaps it was the nature of the award, or both, but the general's speech, delivered haltingly with long pauses, animated the words Duty, Honor, Country, and what emerged was the image of a noble life lived sacrificially for a just and worthy cause.

War was certainly part of MacArthur's address, as was the absolute necessity of victory over a nation's enemies. "Always victory," were his words, but on this day, the rigors, hardships, and sacrifices of war were presented as transformative agents and enablers for a higher purpose. Viewed this way, war is a furnace that sears Duty, Honor, Country into an officer's soul, changing an ordinary life into a noble life that is embodied in the character of an officer and gentleman (and today an officer and lady.) MacArthur's speech also praised the nobility of the American soldier. He said, "When I think of his patience under adversity, of his courage under fire, and of his modesty in victory, I am filled with an emotion of admiration I cannot put into words."

On that long ago day in May, the general gave his heart voice, and with deep emotion, he repeated throughout his speech Duty, Honor, Country like an officer counting cadence. In a sense, he was counting cadence, as he marched through a life lived in dedication to a cause, in awe of the institution at West Point, in admiration of the American soldier, and as a guardian of "this beloved land of culture and ancient descent." The motto bound the man to the institution, the man to his brother soldiers, and the man to the civilization of which he was a sentry, patrolling its walls and repelling all enemies.

To the aged general, Duty, Honor, Country inspired the code by which a military life is lived. He said, "The code which those words perpetuate embraces the highest moral laws and will stand the test of any ethics or philosophies ever promulgated for the uplift of mankind." The code the general said, offers restraint "from the things that are wrong." Most important is the requirement the code places on all soldiers, and that is sacrifice. MacArthur said, "The soldier above all other men, is required to practice the greatest act of religious training – sacrifice." Therefore, the motto and the code it inspires are sacred commitments.

MacArthur's speech was spiritual and aspirational. He said, "Duty, Honor, Country: Those three hallowed words reverently dictate what you ought to be, what you can be, what you will be. They are your rallying points: to build courage when courage seems to fail; to regain faith when there seems to be little cause for faith; to create hope when hope becomes forlorn." Hearing these words were the Corps of Cadets, wearing their gray dress tunics and sitting ramrod straight in precisely arranged rows of chairs. As the general gazed upon their ranks, he referenced a word often heard in the Bible, "leaven." He told the cadets, "You are the leaven which binds together the entire fabric of our national system of defense. From your ranks come the great captains who hold the Nation's destiny in their hands the moment the war tocsin sounds. The long gray line has never failed us."

Duty, Honor, Country is like the breaking curl of an ocean wave, pushing the lives of its adherents toward a noble shore. The motto's power to enliven, enrich, and transform the lives of ordinary men and women into extraordinary individuals is astonishing yet, like the curl represents only a fraction of a wave's power, so it is with the motto. The true power of a wave comes from a lifting up of water from the vast depths of the sea, and likewise the true power of Duty, Honor, Country comes from a lifting up of the Spirit of God from the unfathomable vastness of eternity.

In a speech on June 6, 1984, President Ronald Reagan standing on the cliffs of Normandy, France to commemorate the 40th anniversary of the D-Day invasion, eloquently spoke eternity into the words, Duty, Honor, Country. Addressing veterans of the invasion, the president said:

"You all knew that some things are worth dying for. One's country is worth dying for, and democracy is worth dying for, because it's the most deeply honorable form of government ever devised by man. All of you loved liberty. All of you were willing to fight tyranny, and you knew the people of your countries were behind you.

"The Americans who fought here that morning knew word of the invasion was spreading through the darkness back home. They thought – or felt in their hearts, though they couldn't know in fact – that in Georgia they were filling the churches at 4 a.m., in Kansas they were kneeling on their porches and praying, and in Philadelphia they were ringing the Liberty Bell.

"Something else helped the men of D-day: their rock hard belief that Providence would have a great hand in the events that would unfold here; that God was an ally in this great cause. And so, the night before the invasion, when Colonel Wolverton asked his parachute troops to kneel with him in prayer he told them: Do not bow your heads, but look up so you can see God and ask His blessing in what we're about to do. Also that night, General Matthew Ridgway on his cot, listening in the darkness for the promise God made to Joshua: ``I will not fail thee nor forsake thee."

These are the things that impelled them; these are the things that shaped the unity of the Allies."

"These things" of which Reagan spoke are the character and spirit of a free people and a moral civilization, who refuse to live under the threat of tyranny and death, because they have been given the promise of life and liberty. Duty, Honor, Country is the motto of this civilization's warriors, and Iesus Hominum Salvator (Latin for Jesus Savior of men and by extension all humankind) is the motto of that civilization's free and moral citizens.

Iesus Hominum Salvator is the power of the vastness of eternity, the dwelling place of God, come to into the world. It is the power that lifts individuals, families, communities, nations, and civilizations from the grimy bondage of selfishness, sin and death to the freedom of selfless virtue and life. It is the power that undergirds Duty, Honor, Country, and gives the motto its meaning and purpose. Throughout the thousands of years of human civilization, no three words have so shaped, guided, and ennobled a people. Iesus Hominum Salvator is the motto of Western civilization.

Iesus Hominum Salvator is the power that built Europe's great medieval cathedrals. It is the strength of young muscled Roman Christians, who in the 2nd Century dug the catacombs outside the city to enable the church to worship in times of persecution. When Roman Christians scratched Iesus Hominum Salvator into the earthen walls of their underground chapels, they could scarcely imagine that one day those words would be chiseled into the stones and etched into the stained-glass windows of magnificent cathedrals.

Iesus Hominum Salvator is the courage and spirit of adventure that is the foundation of America. On November 11, 1620, Puritan Pilgrims aboard the Mayflower, floating in what would become Boston Harbor, signed the Compact named after the ship. It reads in part: "Having undertaken for the Glory of God, and Advancement of the Christian Faith, and the Honour of our King and Country, a Voyage to plant the first Colony in the northern Parts of *Virginia*; Do by these Presents, solemnly and mutually, in the Presence of God and one another, covenant and combine ourselves together into a civil Body Politick."[20] The language is awkward to modern ears, but the intent is clear: they pledged themselves to form a government pleasing to God. Today in Washington, D.C., the seat of the U.S. government, the Washington Monument towers over the city, and the tip of this soaring obelisk is inscribed with the words "Laus Deo" (Praise be to God). The Pilgrims could have never imagined how God would bless their courage and spirit of adventure.

Iesus Hominum Salvator is the foundation of the moral code that ended the Atlantic slave trade and precipitated America's Civil War to end slavery. Moral opposition to African slavery in America originated in Christian churches. MacArthur said Duty, Honor, Country inspires "The code …[that]… embraces the highest moral laws and will stand the test of any ethics or philosophies ever promulgated for the uplift of mankind." West Point's moral code to which MacArthur referred is a whole cloth adoption of the moral code handed down to all humankind through Moses and Jesus Christ. It is the moral code from the Bible that teaches the highest ethics, all of which are grounded in the Christian virtues of faith, hope, and love, and the virtue that characterizes all noble lives, which is humility.

Iesus Hominum Salvator is the compassion that in 1865 created The Salvation Army, whose mission "is to preach the gospel of Jesus Christ and to meet human needs in His name without discrimination." That same compassion fuels countless Christian missions that care for the homeless, the addicted, the bruised and battered, the forgotten, the neglected, and the abandoned, because Christ is compassionate.

Iesus Hominum Salvator is the mercy that in the 19th Century reformed prisons in England and America. In 1812, Elizabeth Fry, a Quaker, visited women and children imprisoned in London's Newgate Prison. The overcrowded, unsanitary, and inhumane conditions launched her life's work of mercy and led to a movement to treat prisoners humanely. The source of her mercy was planted in her heart 14 years before that visit. In February 1798, she said, "Today I felt there is a God … to me [that] was like a refreshing shower on parched up earth."[21]

Iesus Hominum Salvator is the love that led 1st Century Christians to frequent garbage dumps outside cities in search of unwanted infants abandoned by their Roman parents.[22] From this beginning, Christians went on to found orphanages, hospitals, and schools not only in the West, but in every corner of the world! Today, Samaritan's Purse, along with hundreds of Christian charities and thousands of churches continue the work.

Iesus Hominum Salvator is the light that sparked a thirst for biblical knowledge, and this spark ignited a desire for knowledge in all things, because through Christ all things were created. From this beginning, the world's great universities were founded: Harvard (Puritan), Yale (Puritan), Princeton (Presbyterian), Oxford (various Christian orders ca. 1096), Cambridge (Christian leaders in 1209), St. Andrews, Scotland (founded in 1413 to teach Christian theology),[23] and the Sorbonne (associated with the cathedral school at Notre Dame, 1150), among others. In fact, Europe's greatest universities trace their origins to the Roman Catholic Church. Should there be any doubt that Iesus Hominum Salvator motivated the development of higher education, the words of Princeton University's first president, the Reverend Jonathan Dickinson, removes all doubt. He said, "Curse be all learning that is contrary to the cross of Christ."[24]

Iesus Hominum Salvator is the power, courage, spirit of adventure, morality, compassion, mercy, love, charity, and light of Western Civilization. These three words written in the blood of countless martyrs, worshiped by the church that refused to bend even when persecuted, prayed over in Holy Scripture, and experienced in the love of Christ transformed the brutal, polytheistic, slaveholding Greco-Roman world. As if these big things were not enough, Iesus Hominum Salvator is found in a multitude of small things.

Iesus Hominum Salvator is typically abbreviated IHS, denoting the first three letters of Jesus' name as it is spelled in Greek: iota (I), eta (H) and Σ (sigma). Similarly, the first two letters of the Greek spelling of Christ are X (chi) and P (rho), and these are combined to give the chi-rho cross (☧) that represents IHS. Both the cross and the initials are so widespread and common throughout the West that they are hardly noticed.

Church buildings, stained glass windows, altars, communion tables, offering plates, hymnals, and banners – it's no surprise that churches, both Catholic and Protestant, have incorporated the cross and IHS into all aspects of the church environment. The West's cemeteries are filled with headstones engraved with IHS and crosses, not only the chi-rho cross, but crosses in a multitude of styles. Then there are cross and IHS jewelry – necklaces, rings, pins, and earrings to mention a few. Art of all types – paintings, tapestries, sculpture, and architecture – from 1st Century to Medieval to Renaissance to Modern feature the cross and IHS. Even mundane things – napkins, stationery, greeting cards, and the list could on – are stamped with crosses and IHS.

Yet a listing of big things and small things inspired by Iesus Hominum Salvator still does not capture the essence of the words. Similarly, MacArthur struggled to capture the essence of Duty, Honor, Country. He was an old man in 1962, when he addressed the cadets, and reflecting upon those words, he said, "Unhappily, I possess neither that eloquence of diction, that poetry of imagination, nor that brilliance of metaphor to tell you all that they mean." He then gave a lengthy description of how Duty, Honor, Country shapes character. Regarding the motto, he said, "They create in your heart a sense of wonder, the unfailing hope of what next, and the joy and inspiration of life. They teach you in this way to be an officer and gentleman."

For MacArthur, West Point was both a real place and a spiritual place. It was a historical place and an eternal place, where the physical and eternal are connected and given life through the words, Duty, Honor, Country. On that day in 1962, the old general was marching with the "long gray line that never fails," and he expected that soon he would "cross the river" [a biblical reference to the Jordan River] to eternity. Two years later, MacArthur died. In 1969, his widow, Jean, returned to West Point to dedicate a monument in his honor.

If the lesser motto of Duty, Honor, Country so speaks to the heart of a general that it connects the physical to the eternal, then surely the superior motto of Iesus Hominum Salvator so speaks to men and women that it connects real lives to eternity and the Lord God, who dwells there. As West Point connected the general to a higher purpose and calling so the church connects all humankind to God, who is the source of meaning and purpose. Duty, Honor, Country defines West Point and is the moral code of the nation's warrior. Iesus Hominum Salvator defines the church and is the holy code of life itself.

This three-word declaration is responsible for all the big things – the power, courage, spirit of adventure, morality, compassion, mercy, love, charity, and light of Western Civilization that were described above, and this declaration likewise makes possible all the small things that are adorned by the cross and IHS. Iesus Hominum Salvator defines us as persons and as Western people. It is the source of the power and nobility expressed in Duty, Honor, Country. Just as these words are etched into the U.S. military's home at West Point, so too are the words Iesus Hominum Salvator etched into the nations that are the West's home.

Of course, particularly today, there are unbelievers. There have always been doubters. In Jerusalem at the time of Jesus' resurrection, there were many who denied his resurrection. Yet the gospel message spread across the 1st Century world with amazing speed, sweeping aside all idols and gods that the ancients worshiped. Despite centuries of persecution, a civilization transformed by Iesus Hominum Salvator emerged. Today's doubters, scoffers, and those hostile to Christians seem to be on the ascendancy and light of Christianity dimming. Many say the faith is old and outdated for the 21st Century. Christianity they say is in the twilight of its relevancy.

In this Western twilight, General MacArthur's words to the candidates that long ago day speak to our hearts. Reflecting on his life, the motto, and West Point, he said, "The shadows are lengthening for me. The twilight is here. My days of old have vanished - tone and tints. They have gone glimmering through the dreams of things that were. Their memory is one of wondrous beauty, watered by tears and coaxed and caressed by the smiles of yesterday. I listen then, but with thirsty ear, for the witching melody of faint bugles blowing reveille, of far drums beating the long roll."

"In my dreams I hear again the crash of guns, the rattle of musketry, the strange, mournful mutter of the battlefield. But in the evening of my memory I come back to West Point. Always there echoes and re-echoes: Duty, Honor, Country."

Today, men and women of Western nations are listening with thirsty ear. In this twilight, we long for the words that will revive our memories – their tone and tint – and to hear the motto of our ancestors so that our minds might be stirred to dream again of being courageous, adventurous, virtuous, moral, and noble gentlemen and gentlewomen. In this evening of our civilization, let us return to the church sanctuary for there within those hallowed and sacred walls echoes and re-echoes: Iesus Hominum Salvator.

"So faith comes from hearing, and hearing through the word of Christ." And, with our motto on our lips and in our hearts, we approach the centuries-long, unbroken line of noble saints, and as we take our place among their ranks, the motto greets our listening ear and fills our beating heart: Iesus Hominum Salvator. Jesus Savior of Mankind (HIS)

Chapter 10: The Sacraments

Jesus, full of the Holy Spirit, left the Jordan and was led by the Spirit into the wilderness, [2] where for forty days he was tempted by the devil. He ate nothing during those days, and at the end of them he was hungry.

[3] The devil said to him, "If you are the Son of God, tell this stone to become bread."

[4] Jesus answered, "It is written: 'Man shall not live on bread alone.'" (Luke 4:1-4)

These verses in Luke capture the tension of being human. Jesus was hungry. He had not eaten for a long time. Yet it was the Holy Spirit, who had put him in this predicament. The Spirit of God led Jesus into the wilderness, where there was nothing to sustain his mortal life, and the reason for his journey was spiritual. In this situation, we clearly see the humanity and the divinity of Jesus, and by extension we are composed of a similar character, being at once both temporal, mortal creatures, who are also eternal. Both we and Jesus experience temptation.

Sensing his human weakness of hunger, Satan tempted Jesus, presenting him with a false choice: "If you are the Son of God, tell this stone to become bread." Whether or not he turned the stone to bread, Jesus remained the Son of God and had no reason to justify or prove himself to refute evil. In fact, no action at all was required. Therefore, Jesus merely stated the obvious tension of the human condition. We are mortal and hunger for bread, and we are spirit and hunger for God. Jesus said to Satan in the wilderness encounter, "Man shall not live on bread alone." This is both a command and a statement of fact. As a statement of fact, it means we are not merely mortal, but eternal, and eternal creatures cannot live on bread alone. We must live on bread and things of the spirit that come from the Spirit of Our Creator. As a command, Jesus' statement means: don't be fooled. You are more than bone and flesh. Therefore, don't try to satisfy the desires of your heart with bread alone. It won't work.

In the sacraments of baptism and communion, Christians are stating to the world, we are not merely mortal, but we are spirit too and in both body and spirit, we belong to Our Creator and Savior. Since we are both body and spirit, it is not surprising that baptism and communion beautifully fuse the physical with the spiritual, the mortal with the eternal. In baptism, water washes the body to symbolize the washing away of sins for entering into a new spiritual life. Christ was baptized; therefore we are baptized too. In communion, bread and wine physically feed the body to spiritually symbolize Jesus' body and blood sacrificed for our sins. Through communion, we remember Christ's death and resurrection and are spiritually renewed as a person and as a community of fellow believers. In the sacraments, the Spirit of God ministers to the human condition both in body and spirit, and this body–spirit tension of being human is transformed from fear to joy. At last, we know that we "do not live by bread alone, but by every word that comes from the mouth of the Lord." (Deuteronomy 8:3) Our mortal spirit is in communion with the Spirit of Our Creator.

The section below takes us to a time when evil reigned in a nation that has played a central role in the shaping of Western Civilization. In the wilderness, evil presented Jesus with a false choice. In this nation, evil afforded no choices, false or otherwise. Evil told the nation, the church, and the people that man lives only by bread alone, and to contradict evil and claim otherwise came at a high cost, including death. How this story ended and what it means for 21st Century Westerners is told below.

* * *

From 1st Century Jerusalem to Paris, April 1, 1977

Steel gray clouds and blustery winds of the Parisian winter were in full retreat, revealing a calm blue sky. In Le Jardin des Tuileries, warm rays of a spring sun coaxed tender buds from stark and bare trees lining the garden's paths. Beyond the garden at the Louvre's entrance, tourists queued, patiently waiting their turn to see treasures of Western art, and on the Seine, the day's first tour boat glided past the Ile de Cité. In the police station of the nearby 9th Arrondissement, the phone rang. The sergeant on-duty answered.

A husky male voice blasted from the phone. "J'ai trouvé les têtes des rois de judah!" ("I found the heads of the Kings of Judah!"),

"Quoi?"

"J'ai trouvé les têtes des rois de judah!"

The sergeant hesitated for a moment, scowled, and then abruptly hung up. It was April 1st and he was in no mood for an April Fool's joke.

Moments later the phone rang again. This voice was calmer, more cultured. The caller said he was the manager of France's Bank of Foreign Trade. The sergeant listened as the manager explained that the bank was enlarging its basement, and just this morning, behind a plastered wall, workers had made a startling discovery. There was a concealed chamber, containing 21 carved limestone heads that appeared to have been cut from the shoulders of large statues. The manager said that he was a student of history and particularly the French Revolution. He was certain these 21 heads were from the original 28 statues of the Kings of Judah that had graced the outside walls of Notre Dame Cathedral. For almost two centuries, they had been missing. Today, he believed they were found!

In the autumn of 1793, the French Revolution was over four years old. The initial exhilaration of opposing the king had passed, and the dream of establishing a government of Liberty, Equality, and Fraternity was only that – a dream. France was now entering a nightmare. The Reign of Terror was underway.

On October 14, 1793, Marie Antoinette, the last Queen of France, was convicted of high treason by the Revolutionary Tribunal. Two days later, she was executed by guillotine in what today is called the Place de la Concorde. Her death did not slate Parisians' thirst for blood vengeance. Later that month, a mob swarmed onto the plaza in front of Notre Dame Cathedral, howling for more noble blood. With no actual royalty available, the mob's wrath turned toward the cathedral itself.

As far back as 1230, limestone statues of the Kings of Judah stood solemn and silent watch, observing more than 500 years of French history from their niches in the cathedral's outside wall above the plaza. The stone crowns and flowing carved robes marked them as kings. The image of any royalty stoked the mob's anger. Believing these were French kings, they tied ropes around the statues and pulled until they toppled to the pavement. They found a guillotine, and one by one, the stone Kings of Judah were drug to the killing machine and beheaded. With each bloodless drop of the blade, the mob shrieked in vengeful delight as the limestone heads thumped onto the pavement. Amid the chaos, the heads mysteriously disappeared, and remained missing until France's Bank of Foreign Trade decided it needed a larger basement. [25, 26]

Restless and angry, the mob that October night in 1793 looked at the cathedral and saw one thing and one thing only: an institution. To the mob, the church was no different than say the Ministry of Justice. The king, his judges, sheriffs, and jailers meted out justice. The list of crimes was lengthy, and because poverty was widespread so were property crimes such as theft.

Judgments and sentences were handed out in a charged atmosphere that boiled out of control on July 14, 1789. On that date, the Bastille prison was stormed. Ironically, only seven prisoners were held in the Bastille at the time of the attack, but that didn't matter. The mob was actually after the ammunition that was stored within the walls. The ammunition would fuel the revolution, but more importantly, a message was being sent: the king's institutions and the king himself were not safe. Four years later, this same message was being delivered at another institution: the church as represented by Notre Dame Cathedral. The mob's attack on Notre Dame raises an important question with which Westerners continue to struggle: is the church merely an institution? Our answer to this question depends upon our answer to a seminal antecedent question: does man live by bread alone?

The mob's beheading of kingly statues on that long ago night was their answer. The church is merely an institution, and in 18th Century France, it was the king's institution. The French church was supported by a tax, bishops and well-placed priests exercised civil and political authority under the king's watchful eye. Therefore, a strong case could be made that the church is merely an institution, but if we look deeper into Notre Dame's past and indeed all of Europe's great cathedrals, a different story emerges. It is a story of spirit and worldly temptation with parallels in Jesus' story in the wilderness, where the physical and temporal are in tension with the spiritual and eternal, and choices must be made.

Notre Dame was constructed between 1163 and 1235. It was part of a massive church building campaign that swept Europe. In the hundred years, between 1170 and 1270, more than 500 great churches were built in France alone! They were built in the Gothic style that first appeared with the restoration of the St. Denis Abbey outside of Paris. A new building technique, the flying buttress, allowed thinner and much taller walls to be built. Gone were the massively thick stone pillars that characterized earlier Romanesque churches. Medieval architects could now reach heights never before achieved. The Cathedral at Chartres stands at roughly 30 stories, but even that great height is topped by the Strasbourg Cathedral at 40 stories! The goal was to achieve the tallest structure possible to create the illusion that the church was reaching to heaven itself, linking the mortal to the eternal. Father Suger, the abbot of St. Denis Abbey, where the grand Gothic style originated, described his reaction to his church as follows:

I seem to find myself, as it were, in some strange part of the universe which was neither wholly of the baseness of the earth nor wholly of the serenity of heaven, but by the grace of God I seemed lifted in a mystic manner from this lower towards the upper sphere.[27]

It wasn't simply the height of the churches that made the abbot's soul feel lifted upward. Light played an important role too. With the advent of the flying buttress, windows for the first time could be more strategically placed without diminishing structural integrity. Thus, marvelous windows were designed with brilliant colors, and Gothic cathedrals are known for their large and striking rose windows. Worshipers in the nave looking upward at the bright blues, golds, and reds of a rose window are inclined to feel that God in heaven has descended and in His glory is shining on them. Church historian, Bruce Shelley described the experience as follows:

Artists used brilliant colors – crimson, blue, purple, ruby – to tell the story of redemption from creation to the Last Judgment. Worshipers, then, could ponder the sacrifice of Isaac, the crossing of the Red Sea, the birth of Jesus, or Saint Anthony's struggle with devils. The total effect was breathtaking. As the evening sun cast its warm enchanting rays upon the cold gray stone, even the cobbler from his pew could sense his kinship with Moses, Isaiah, Jesus, Paul, Augustine, and Benedict.[28]

And, if the worshiper missed the message in the windows, then the cross-shaped footprint of the cathedral itself shouted to him – redemption! Death has been conquered! Eternity awaits mortal man.

Notre Dame and the great European cathedrals are a triumphal harnessing of human reason and ingenuity to express divine revelation, and the revelation is this: God dwells in us through faith in Christ Jesus. By faith, our sins are forgiven, and we are lifted in a mystic manner, where we sense his presence, suspended like Fr. Suger between the "baseness of the earth [and]… the serenity of heaven." Winston Churchill said, "We shapc our buildings, and thereafter, they shape us." Notre Dame was clearly designed to shape generation upon generation spiritually. The cathedral was much more than the king's church.

Europe's great cathedrals stand as witnesses that the church is no mere institution. Churches, whether magnificent cathedrals inlaid with marvelous stained glass or the humblest clapboard country church are physical locations that house the spiritual Kingdom of God. We ourselves are no different. Whether tall or short, fat or skinny, homely or handsome, as Christians, we are the physical locations that house the spiritual Kingdom of God. We are citizens of Christ Jesus' kingdom that originates in eternity and encompasses the past, present, and future of human history. It was the fusing of the physical with the spiritual that lifted Fr. Suger in a mystical manner, and it is that same fusion that enabled generations of poor cobblers "from his pew … [to]… sense his kinship with Moses, Isaiah, Jesus, Paul, Augustine, and Benedict." The cornerstone of the physical-spiritual church is Jesus Christ who was tempted and in his hour of temptation told us that man does not live by bread alone, but by the Spirit of God.

As citizens of the Kingdom of God, we celebrate and commemorate the spiritual with ceremonies involving the physical: the sacraments of baptism and communion. Baptism symbolizes a spiritual rebirth that makes a bold and shocking claim: the baptized person is dead to sin and risen to new eternal life in Christ Jesus. In infant baptism, the parents are making this claim on behalf of the child, who then affirms that claim when they are older. Of course, even after baptism, people do sinful and immoral things. A baptized person is never perfect, but the person is redeemed and has a new spirit, and the Apostle Paul described for us this new spirit.

14 *For those who are led by the Spirit of God are the children of God.* 15 *The Spirit you received does not make you slaves, so that you live in fear again; rather, the Spirit you received brought about your adoption to sonship. And by him we cry, "Abba Father."* 16 *The Spirit himself testifies with our spirit that we are God's children.* 17 *Now if we are children, then we are heirs—heirs of God and co-heirs with Christ, if indeed we share in his sufferings in order that we may also share in his glory.* (Romans 8:14-17)

Baptism is a once in a lifetime event. A baptized person has no needed to be re-baptized. When we stray and sin, we only need to repent and to remind us to repent, Jesus has given us the sacrament of communion. The Apostle Paul's words that are used to begin the communion ceremony confirm that Christ's body (the bread) is the sustenance of life, and Christ's blood (the wine) is the source of our redemption and entry into new life. Paul's words are:

23 *For I received from the Lord what I also passed on to you: The Lord Jesus, on the night he was betrayed, took bread,* 24 *and when he had given thanks, he broke it and*

said, "This is my body, which is for you; do this in remembrance of me." [25] *In the same way, after supper he took the cup, saying, "This cup is the new covenant in my blood; do this, whenever you drink it, in remembrance of me."* [26] *For whenever you eat this bread and drink this cup, you proclaim the Lord's death until he comes.* (1 Corinthians 12: 23-26)

Clearly, the church is no mere institution. It is a physical outpost of the spiritual Kingdom of God that was established by Jesus Christ, and commemorated and celebrated in the sacraments. But, as a physical outpost, it is run by living and breathing people, who are not perfect. Christ breathes a new spirit into anyone, who seeks him, repents, and follows his teachings. Yet because we are human, we are still tempted and often weak. When temptation comes, we often don't imitate Jesus in the wilderness, where he eschewed temptation and rebuked Satan. We often give into temptation, and thus provide the opportunity for naysayers to point to the church and proclaim that it is a mere institution. Over the centuries, the church has waxed and waned sometimes being a good reflection of Christ's spiritual kingdom and others not. Today, Westerners are quick to point out the church's failures, while ignoring her faith, charity, forbearance, and love that has shaped our civilization. Such shaping was not accomplished by a mere institution, but only by an outpost of the Kingdom of God.

What really happened on that long ago October night in 1793 was the Parisian mob didn't attack an institution. They attacked an outpost of the Kingdom of God and in doing so they proclaimed, not only is the church a mere institution, but they declared that man does live by bread alone. Hence, there is no God, no kingdom, no Savior, and no Holy Spirit. In fact, the mob sided with Satan when he tempted Jesus, telling him to prove himself by turning stones into bread. What are the consequences of rejecting God and concluding that humankind is merely mortal? It is called the Reign of Terror.

The Jacobin radicals believed that, if the goals and ideals of the French Revolution were to advance, then the church had to be brought to heel. Therefore, one of the first acts of the Estates-General in 1789 was to strip the church of money and property and to remove the Vatican from any say in placement and advancement of priests and bishops. The state controlled the church, but it wanted even more. The state coveted God's place in the hearts of priests and in the heart of the church herself so the revolutionary government passed a new draconian law.

The Civil Constitution of the Clergy required all priests to swear a loyalty oath to the state. The state's oath superseded the clergy's oath to God, and initially, roughly three-fourths refused to swear the oath. Penalties for refusing varied and given the upheaval of the revolution, enforcement wasn't uniform. Withholding the state's salary to priests, who declined the oath, was one of the milder punishments; death was the extreme and many priests, monks, and nuns were executed. But, the revolutionary government coveted more than control over clergy, the radicals sought to remove God entirely from the church. To accomplish this goal, all contemplative monastic orders were abolished and the church was ordered to restrict her activities to education and social services. Nuns, monks, and priests were guillotined. Mass still could be celebrated, but with contemplative activities outlawed the heart of God touching the heart of humankind, was now forbidden under French law. To make such anti-church, anti-God measures palatable at least to Parisians, the Jacobins whipped up anger against the church to the point that the mob that October night defiled Notre Dame Cathedral and beheaded statues.

None of these events surprised Edmund Burke (1729-97), a philosopher, and member of the British Parliament. He was an early and keen observer of the French Revolution. In *Reflections on the Revolution in France*, he wrote, "It seems to me that this new ecclesiastical establishment is intended only to be temporary, and preparatory to the utter abolition, under any of its forms, of the Christian religion." Burke did not believe for a moment that the French Revolution was simply about establishing a new constitutional form of government. He understood events in France to be driven by a "literary cabal" of so-called philosophers of the Enlightenment, who were intent on the destruction of Christianity and the triumph of atheism.

Events during the Reign of Terror quickly confirmed Burke's view of the French Revolution. By mandate of the state, atheism was imposed and Christianity was slated for extinction. The "Cult of Reason" was France's first state sponsored godless religion that was promoted as a replacement for Christianity. Inspired by the writings of Rousseau, the goal of the cult was perfection of humankind through the attainment of truth and liberty.[29] However, with truth, liberty, and reason subject to human interpretation, it was a cult of vanity, not reason. Next came the "Cult of the Supreme Being" that was the brain-child of Robespierre, who believed that people, e.g., the masses, needed to believe in some sort of supreme being, if for no other reason than to maintain social order. Thus, the supreme being cult was born. The two cults competed to become the new state religion. Both were banned by Napoleon in 1802, and the last vestiges of the Reign of Terror came to an end. [30]

Does man live by bread alone? It's such a simple question, but how it is answered leads to either heaven or hell. Our participation in the sacraments confirms our choice. We choose heaven, and whether communion and baptism take place amid the splendor of a grand Gothic cathedral or in an unadorned country church, we are lifted in a mystic manner, because the

Holy Spirit is present. Thus, the sacraments are sacred, and the church is no mere institution. "Man does not live on bread alone, but on every word that comes from the mouth of the Lord." (Deuteronomy 8:3)

Chapter 11: Benediction

And God saw that it was good.
And God blessed them. (Genesis 1:10, 28)

These verses are Creation's benediction. Benediction is derived from Latin "bene" meaning good or well, and "diction" meaning to speak; literally to speak good as in a blessing. In Creation God spoke goodness and blessed all that he had made, including humankind. In fact, the phrase, "And God saw that it was good," was repeated after every act of creation. Hanging the sun, moon, and stars, gathering the waters to form dry land and the seas, and breathing life in every creature upon the earth, including humans, God proclaimed it all good. In particular he blessed men and women, saying:

So God created man in his own image,
in the image of God he created him;
male and female he created them.
28 *And God blessed them.* (Genesis 1: 27-28)

Benedictions are the concluding good words and blessing before worshipers leave the sanctuary and take up their roles in the everyday world. Is it possible that God in the Genesis creation account was proclaiming goodness and blessing Adam and Eve, because he knew what was coming next, which was rejection of him, sin, fear, hiding, and expulsion from Eden? Well, of course, he knew. He knew what lay beyond Eden's East Gate which was the everyday world in which we live. In giving Creation's benediction, God was telling Adam and Eve, and by extension all of us that even though we live outside of Eden, the blessing remains. God has not forgotten or given up on us. While we cannot return to the perfect fellowship with God that we had in Eden, we can know God and experience his presence. In fact, Revelation chapters 21 and 22 describe the new heavenly Eden.

But what about this side of heaven, the earthly side, where does the Eden-like presence of God happen? It happens in worship either in private or with others, and the Order of Worship is our template for worship and returning to God's presence. Before we step into the sanctuary or kneel in private, we have at least an inkling that God is there and that he intends good for us, and our inkling is the remnant of the benediction that God placed in the human heart at Creation. When we act on this inkling, we hear the Call to Worship (Chapter 4) which was God's call to Adam and Eve, "Where are you? (Genesis 1:9). By our presence we are answering, "Here I am." But, we have returned to God's presence as sinners. Therefore, we participate in the Confession of Sin & Assurance of Pardon (Chapter 5), and Jesus says, "Has no one condemned you? Neither do I condemn you; go, and from now on sin no more. (John 8:10-11) In the Pastoral Prayer (Chapter 6), we fellowship with God, presenting to him our most intimate needs and asking him to "hear from heaven and act." (1 Kings 8:32) Because we are forgiven and God hears our prayers, we celebrate in the Anthem (Chapter 7), and with King David, we shout, "I will awaken the dawn." (Psalm 57:8). During the Anthem, we have the opportunity to make our offering. With the widow in the Temple, who gave her two mites (Mark 6:3-4), as an example of sacrificial giving, the Offertory (Chapter 8) is our opportunity to make our offering in faith with humility and dignity. In the Sermon, Proclamation of God's Word (Chapter 9), our faith is nurtured, because "faith comes from hearing and hearing through the word of Christ." (Romans 10:17) The central message of Christianity is this: Iesus

Hominum Salvator (Jesus, the Savior of humankind). In the Sacraments (Chapter 10) of communion and baptism, we affirm that "man shall not live by bread alone." (Luke 4:4), and with this affirmation we enter into the deepest experience of God. Now, only the Benediction is left. Once the Benediction is pronounced, the rigors, challenges, sorrows, delights, victories, rewards, loneliness, and celebrations of the everyday world awaits. Therefore, just as God pronounced the benediction on Adam and Eve to face the world beyond Eden's East Gate so we too receive those good words and blessing, as we live life beyond the church doors.

With the words of the benediction in our hearts, we can experience God in everyday life, but, like the 1st Century Christians in Rome, we should expect no help, encouragement, or reinforcement in this endeavor from the prevailing popular culture. Today we confront a Western civilization that is hostile to Christians. Godless Westerners are like reformed cigarette smokers. Reformed smokers are the most aggressive and belligerent enforcers of no smoking. They've given up the habit, why can't you? So, it is with godless Westerners. They've given up Christianity, why can't you?

Well, there are two reasons why we can't give up. First is truth. Having experienced God and the forgiveness of sin through Christ, Christians know truth – truth about who we are, who God is, and the truth about the devastating consequences of a sinful society. These consequences are hopelessness, loneliness, violence, exploitation, and injustice, and these characteristics are rampant in the West today, which brings up the second reason Christian's can't give up on Christianity. Christians are "the salt of the earth" (Matthew 5:13), meaning that Western civilization depends upon Christians civilizing society. Western civilization today desperately needs truth and the civilizing influence of Christianity, because we are confronted with choices that will determine the future of humanity. Will the future be a benediction – "and God saw that it was good" and "God blessed them"? Or, will the future be a curse – "they have given themselves over to sensuality so as to indulge in every kind of impurity, and they are full of greed"? (Ephesians 4:19)

This question is not a rarified academic musing, but a concrete and serious question that impacts all of our lives, as the following story illustrates. Below you will meet men with god-like power; power that the world has never before seen. Decisions about how to use this power must be made, and what will be basis for making those decisions? Will it be the good words of God's blessings that are based on 4,000 years of Judeo-Christianity or Western barbarism as described by the Apostle Paul in Ephesians? The consequences of this question are so grave that presidents of the United States have been alerted to the danger. Now, let's begin the story.

* * *

From 1st Century Jerusalem to San Francisco, 1976

Dr. Herbert Boyer leaned back in his desk chair and surveyed his cluttered desk. He reached for the stack of charts, tables, and summaries prepared by his graduate students and post-docs, tapped the papers on the desk to straighten them, and set the stack aside. His research at the University of California San Francisco was going well – quite well in fact. There is it, he said to himself, picking up the galley proof of his and Dr. Stanley Cohen's latest peer-reviewed scientific publication. Their research was attracting a lot of attention. Research grants to support their work were now much easier to get than when they first started out, but with the attention came unwanted distractions.

It was just three years earlier in 1973, that he and Dr. Cohen had successfully transferred frog RNA into a strain of *E. coli* bacteria. Their transfer technique was reproducible, and they were pioneers in the emerging field of gene transfer. It was an area of research that held great potential for developing new medical therapies, and much more. The ability to transfer a gene into *E. coli* or yeast, and have that gene work meant that say a gene that codes for human insulin could be put into *E. coli.* As the bacteria grows and reproduces, the recombinant genetic code would produce human insulin that could be collected, purified, and used to treat patients with Type 1 diabetes.

Dr. Boyer had just settled into reviewing the galley proof, when there was a knock on his office door. "Yes," he said, the frustration evident in his voice. The door opened and a young man wearing a sport coat and tie stepped in.

"Bob Swanson," he said with a boyish grin that matched his youthful appearance.

Dr. Boyer peered at him for moment. "Move those papers and you can have a seat there," he said, pointing to one of the chairs in front of his desk. Swanson cleared the papers and handed the professor his business card. Boyer placed it on the desk and then looked up. "Ten minutes," Boyer said. "That's what we agreed to. And, I'll warn you that my research is what interests me, and I'm not looking for any venture capital. Now, what's on your mind, Mr. Swanson?"

Ten minutes turned into three hours, and during that time a world-class biotechnology company was born. Swanson, the venture capitalist, and Boyer, the scientist, decided to name it Genentech. One of the company's early products was human insulin. Today, Genentech is owned by The Roche Group, and the company is a leader in pharmaceuticals. From 1976 to 1990, Dr. Boyer served as vice president of Genentech in addition to continuing in his professorial role at UC San Francisco.[31] In

1986, Dr. Stanley Cohen was awarded the Nobel Prize in Medicine.[32] In 1990, roughly 15 years after Boyer and Cohen's pioneering work with bacteria, the possibility of transferring genes into humans was being seriously considered, and Dr. French Anderson of the National Institutes of Health's Clinical Center believed that a four-year old child named Ashanthi should be the first person to undergo gene therapy.

Ashanthi was born with an incurable genetic immune deficiency called severe combined immune deficiency (SCID). She suffered from constant debilitating infections, because the gene that codes for the enzyme, adenosine deaminase (ADA), was either missing or corrupted. A robust immune system needs ample ADA to boost T-cell count and fight infections. With ADA missing, Ashanthi suffered one infection after another and treatment required continued injections of ADA to beat back the infection. Once the ADA circulating in her body was depleted, and lacking a functional gene to make fresh ADA, a new infection would set in. It was an unending cycle of hospitalizations. By age four, the ADA injections were less effective. Unless a new treatment was found, Ashanthi would likely never reach adulthood.

Dr. Anderson, who was investigating the use of viruses to transfer genes into human cells, believed that Ashanthi could benefit from his work. Medical experimentation on human subjects is controversial, and the fact that Ashanthi was a child further complicated the moral and ethical dilemma. Yet Dr. Anderson, believing that Ashanthi could benefit greatly from gene therapy, pressed ahead and received all the necessary approvals to proceed.

Working with a team of researchers and physicians, Dr. Anderson secured a source of the gene that codes for ADA and proceeded to incorporate the ADA gene into a virus. The genetically engineered virus was then injected into Ashanti, and the research team waited. Thankfully, the wait was short. Ashanti's ADA instantly increased! The ADA gene was working, and the little girl experienced few side effects. Today, Ashanthi is an adult, and she will always have the distinction of being the world's first person to successfully receive gene transfer therapy.

Such powerful new technology applied to human genetics rightfully provoked moral and ethical discussion. If gene transfer could be used to heal, it could also be used to harm. What sort of other genes might be transferred to humans that cause them to be less than human? Bioengineering human beings, i.e., designer babies, was no longer the stuff of science fiction. The possibility of creating humanoids with characteristics selected by their designers was now very real. This powerful new technology raised moral and bioethical issues that go to the core of what it means to be human and what are the limits that the human genome can or should be manipulated.

To address these issues, President Clinton in 1996 created the National Bioethics Advisory Commission. Subsequent presidents have renamed the commission and expanded its scope, but the work remains unchanged.[33] In 2003, the commission released a major report that summarized its thinking on gene transfer and what it means to be human.

Increasingly, advances in biomedical science and technology raise profound challenges to familiar human practices and ways of thinking, feeling, and acting. It is no wonder, then, that bioethics touches matters close to the core of our humanity: birth and death, body and mind, sickness and health, freedom and dignity are but a few of these. With this in mind the Council has prepared Being Human: Readings from the President's Council on Bioethics, an anthology of works of literature that speak to bioethical dilemmas.[34]

The "Being Human" anthology consists of ten chapters that presents 95 works of literature that includes Shakespeare, Tolstoy, American folk songs, poetry, fiction, and the Bible. The first chapter of the anthology is entitled "The Search for Perfection," and one of the literary works selected for this chapter is an 1843 short story by Nathaniel Hawthorne called "The Birthmark." Hawthorne's short story offers a surprising parallel to Ashanthi's story.

Except for the tiniest of flaws, Ashanthi was born perfectly healthy. In the grand scheme of things, the one thing that she was missing was infinitesimally small. It's so small – a single enzyme out of the roughly 1,300 enzymes in the human body – that perhaps it might not be that important, but it is and to Ashanthi, the one missing thing threatened her life. To fix this one tiny thing, Dr. Anderson and his team of scientists to had change Ashanthi at her core; they had to change a gene. The goal of Dr. Anderson's team was to restore Ashanthi to health to allow her to live into whatever God has planned in her life. Restoration, life, and giving – that is Ashanthi's story. But, what if the motive for changing a person at their core is not goodness, but arrogance, vanity, and selfishness? And, what if the change is not about restoring creation's intended design, but creating your own design for them to satisfy your wants? Hawthorne's "The Birthmark" is just such a story.

The Birthmark is the story of Aylmer, who was a renowned scientist, and his beautiful young wife, Georgiana. Aylmer was devoted to science, and he spent years toiling in his laboratory with great success. His command over nature seemed to know no limit. His first love, and seemingly only love, was science until he met Georgiana. During their courtship, she appeared to be the personification of perfection to Aylmer. Once married, however, he fixated on a tiny flaw, a birthmark on her cheek. They had only been married a short while, when Aylmer remarked, "Georgiana, has it never occurred to you that the mark on your cheek might be removed?"

Her husband's question took her by surprise, and she blushed. She did not perceive the birthmark as a flaw, but as part of her charm. It was an ever so small crimson spot on her left cheek that was in the shape of a tiny human hand. The fact that she saw it as part of her natural charm was not unfounded. Her suitors before she married "were wont to say, that some fairy, at her birth-hour, had laid her tiny hand upon the infant's cheek, and left this impress there, in token of the magic endowments that were to give her such sway over all hearts." Typically, the tiny hand was clearly visible against the "delicate bloom" of her pale skin, but when she blushed it all but disappeared, betraying her inner-most thoughts and emotions. The tiny hand revealed her humanity. It was her charm. It was part of who she was.

But to Aylmer it was not a magical mark left by a fairy. All he saw was a hideous red blemish that he could not get out of his mind. It was an imperfection on an otherwise perfect creature. To Aylmer the "Crimson Hand" was a "frightful object" representing "his wife's liability to sin, sorrow, decay, and death." Moreover, "when they sat together at the evening hearth, his eyes wandered stealthily to her cheek, and beheld, flickering with the blaze of the wood fire, the spectral Hand that wrote mortality, where he would fain have worshipped."

Georgiana lived with Aylmer's disappointed glances until she could take it no more. What pushed her over the edge was when Aylmer begin dreaming about the birthmark and shouting out in his sleep. Late one evening she asked, "My dear Aylmer, have you any recollection of a dream last night, about this odious Hand?" When he replied that he had no memory of any such dream, she fought back tears and told him that in the night he cried out, "It is in her heart now – we must have it out!"

Then, she said, "Reflect, my husband; for by all means I would have you recall that dream."

Aylmer searched his memory and began to piece together the nightmare. With knife in hand, he was poised to cut the Hand from Georgiana's cheek. He quickly discovered it wasn't a superficial mark, and the deeper he cut "the deeper sank the Hand, until at length its tiny grasp appeared to have caught hold of Georgiana's heart; whence, however, her husband was inexorably resolved to cut or wrench it away."

Upon hearing the details of the dream, Georgiana now understood that the Crimson Hand, the spectral Hand, the Hand that represents sin, sorrow, decay, and death had to be removed, not only for the sake of her marriage, but for herself also. She wanted it gone, because she came to recognize it as a "fatal birthmark … which was laid upon me before I came into the world." Aylmer, the brilliant scientist that he was, was certain he could remove it. Georgiana told him, "If there be the remotest possibility of it, let the attempt be made, at whatever risk. Danger is nothing to me; for life – while this hateful mark makes me the object of your horror and disgust – life is a burthen which I would fling down with joy. Either remove this dreadful Hand, or take my wretched life! You have deep science!" Aylmer responded, crying out, "Do not doubt my power" and the plan to remove it was laid.

The next morning, Georgiana entered the outer rooms of her husband's laboratory. These were beautifully decorated, and are best described as a combination library and museum that documented and showcased all of Aylmer's marvelous discoveries. Despite the pleasantness of the rooms, when Georgiana entered she fainted, and Aylmer revived her with wonderful fragrances. Soon, she was alert and comfortable, and Aylmer entertained her with his splendid inventions. At one point he told her "that it was his option to concoct a liquid that should prolong life for years – perhaps interminably – but that it would produce a discord in nature." He called this potion the "Elixir Vitae," and it frightened Georgiana, who said, "It is terrible to possess such power, or even dream of possessing it!"

Aylmer reassured her saying, "Do not mistrust me dearest! Its virtuous potency is yet greater than its harmful one." Having comforted Georgiana, Aylmer disappeared into the inner rooms, where his laboratory was located. Alone in the outer rooms, Georgiana amused herself with her husband's inventions and the books in his library.

Hours passed, and when Aylmer finally emerged from the laboratory, Georgiana was feeling odd. "It was a sensation in the fatal birthmark, not painful, but which induced a restlessness throughout her system." She suspected that her husband had already surreptitiously given her some potion to remove the Hand. Yet she did not ask him about it, nor did she report her symptoms to him. But, she did secretly follow him into the laboratory, and was immediately struck by the inner room's stark bareness, its heat, and gases. From a distance, she watched him work. Gone was the confident and calm scientist. "He was pale as death, anxious, and absorbed, and hung over the furnace as if it depended upon his utmost watchfulness whether the liquid, which was distilling, should be the draught of immortal happiness or misery."

When Aylmer spotted her watching him, he was not pleased. "He rushed towards her, and seized her arm with a gripe [sic] that left the print of his fingers upon it." As he escorted her out of the lab, he admitted to having already given her a potion to remove the birthmark, but it didn't work. He said, "Know then, that this Crimson Hand, superficial as it seems, has clutched its grasp into your being, with a strength of which I had no previous conception." The next treatment option was the "draught" that he was distilling over the furnace, but it was risky. He tells her, "there is danger" in drinking it.

"'Danger? There is but one danger – that this horrible stigma shall be left upon my cheek!" cried Georgiana. 'Remove it! Remove it – whatever be the cost, or we shall both go mad!'"

Aylmer agrees to give her the draught and returned with "a crystal goblet containing a liquor colorless as water, but bright enough to be the draught of immortality." As he handed Georgiana the goblet, he said, "The concoction of the draught has been perfect. Unless all my science has deceived me, it cannot fail."

Georgiana took the goblet and drank the draught. Immediately, she became drowsy, and said, "Now dearest, let me sleep. My earthy senses are closing over my spirit, like the leaves around the heart of a rose, at sunset."

With these words, she fell into a deep stupor. Aylmer hovered over her, watching. The scientist in him observed her with an academic disinterest, as he made mental notes of her response to the draught. But, the husband in him was not so dispassionate. At one point, he bent over and kissed the birthmark, but then "his spirit recoiled." As time passed, she became very pale, but his concern over her paleness was swept aside by the joy of seeing the Crimson Hand fade until it was barely visible. "By heavens, it is neigh well gone!" he said to himself.

Georgiana, still very pale, woke, and gazed into a mirror positioned by Aylmer. "A faint smile flitted over her lips, when she recognized how barely perceptible was now that Crimson Hand." She looked at her husband and murmured, "My poor Aylmer!"

"'Poor? Nay, richest! Happiest! Most favored! exclaimed he. 'My peerless bride, it is successful! You are perfect!'"

"'My poor Aylmer," she repeated, with a more than human tenderness. 'You have aimed loftily! – you have done nobly! Do not repent, that, with so high and pure a feeling, you have rejected the best that earth could offer. Aylmer – dearest Aylmer – I am dying." With these words, Georgiana was gone. As for the Hand, Hawthorne wrote, "As the last crimson tint of the birthmark – that sole token of human imperfection – faded from her cheek, the parting breath of the now perfect woman passed into the atmosphere, and her soul lingering a moment near her husband, took its heavenward flight." Aylmer's science had not failed. It had removed "the spectral Hand that wrote mortality, where he would fain have worshipped." The imperfection was gone and his wife with it.

Georgiana's fictional story parallels Ashanthi's real life story in many ways. Both had the tiniest of physical flaws that resulted from the core of their being. In Georgiana's case, Aylmer said the tiny hand "has clutched its grasp into your being, with a strength of which I had no previous conception." In Ashanthi's case, Dr. Anderson knew it was a single gene, the one that codes for ADA. Both Aylmer and Dr. Anderson's procedures were successful. Aylmer removed the birthmark; Anderson replaced the flawed gene. But here's the difference: Ashanthi's health was restored as intended at creation, and she lived. Georgiana's life was destroyed, because Aylmer was intent on altering her into something that she was never intended to be. The substantive issue is the motive for inventing and using the science in the first place. Motive comes from what is in the human heart, which includes how we understand ourselves, how we view Nature, our belief (or not) in God, our understanding of the immortality of the human soul, and our basis of truth. Hawthorne clearly had all these things in mind when he wrote The Birthmark, which is an examination of the motives of the human heart, and the consequences of those motives on others.

Aylmer and Georgiana are of course fictional, but imagine a world with dozens of medical centers staffed by Aylmers intent on perfecting human beings, and they – not God – will decide what is perfect. It's a world of doom ruled by those who would be god, ruling humanoids created in their image. It's a world so frightening that we prefer not to think about it. Now, imagine dozens of medical centers around the world staffed by scientists and physicians, who desire to restore health by fixing malfunctions so that it works as designed by God. It is two entirely different worlds, and who is better equipped to make decisions about the kind of world in which we live? Christians informed by 4,000 years of Judeo-Christian thought, faith, and practice, or the modern Western barbarians informed only by their lust and greed?

This moral dilemma created by gene transfer is obviously an extreme situation, but the extreme illuminates the everyday common moral landscape in which Westerners now live. What is the moral and ethical basis that guides Western laws and attitudes on marriage, so-called gender fluidity, the sanctity of life, sex outside of marriage, and a range of other issues? The basis of our laws and societal attitudes rest on what we believe to be true, and here is where the extent of Western confusion and depravity are ultimately revealed. The great societal debate in the West in not what is or will be our basis of truth, but whether truth even exists. If truth does not exist, then we have no means of deciding what is right and what is wrong. In a world devoid of truth, only power is left. Those with power will decide what is right or wrong, acceptable or not, legal or illegal. Powerful technologies in the hands of godless immoral people do not bless the world with God's benediction at Creation, but curse it with a blasphemy for they have presumed to be god.

This is the crisis that the West faces, and there are two things that Christian must do to ensure the future is a benediction and not a curse.

First we must understand that the Genesis creation account is central to every aspect of Christianity. Undermine God as Our Creator, then every tenet of the Christian faith becomes wobbly. Darwin published his "Origin of the Species" in the 1850's, which was roughly 170 years ago. For the early 1800's, when his theory was formulated, evolution of the species was cutting edge stuff. But, have you seen a phrenologist lately to read the bumps on your head and give you a diagnosis? Have you had your arm or leg sawed off in the past year because a simple cut became infected and turned into gangrene? Well, that and worse was the state of the West's scientific knowledge when Darwin presented his theory to the Royal Society. Yet, 170 years later the West continues to debate Darwinism has if he presented his paper last week, and sadly far too many Westerners believe the Genesis creation account is totally discredited.

Compounding this dilemma is the Christian response – if there is any response at all. All too often Christians are drawn into debating the age of the earth and fossils. Focusing on such things diverts attention from the true significance of the creation account, which is a loving God, whose creation is good, and filled with people created in his image, who are saved by faith. Because God, as Creator, speaks deeply into the human condition, the creation account is the starting point of Western philosophy, law, and ethics which are the traits needed to give light, insight, and meaning to very difficult issues that confront us, as shown in the stories of Ashanthi and Georgiana.

Second have faith and confidence; live into Creation's benediction. In worship, God's benediction is renewed and likewise our hearts are renewed to enable Christians to be "the salt of the earth" just as we have been for 2,000 years. The

Benediction is God's blessing to all generations. May it fill our hearts in our everyday world, and in doing so move us closer to Eden. Western civilization depends upon it!

Part III: Restored To Who We Can Be

Christ the Mediator

In his eternal purpose it pleased God to choose and ordain the Lord Jesus, his only begotten Son, to be the mediator between God and man. Jesus is the prophet, priest, and king, the head and savior of his church, the heir of all things, and judge of the world. From all eternity God gave him a people to be his seed and to be in time redeemed, called, justified, sanctified, and glorified by him.

Westminster Confession of Faith, Chapter VIII, 6.043

Chapter 12: Love & Justice, Part I

A psalm of David.

I will sing of your love and justice;
to you, Lord, I will sing praise. (Psalm 101:1)

Love and justice. It seems like an incongruous combination. Justice is the correction of injustice. A wrong has happened. There is a victim and a perpetrator, and when the verdict is read, one, the other, or perhaps both are going to be angry. Yet, David put the two together and praised God, because both love and justice come from the Lord God. When we understand that David wrote this psalm, not as a judge but as a king, the incongruity vanishes. This verse is actually a window into the king's heart and his desires for his kingdom. David desired to govern ancient Israel with love and justice, because that's what God desires and we know that David was a man whose heart sought the heart of God. (1 Samuel 13:14)

What of Western leaders today? Is the chief goal of their governance love and justice, or something else? It is something else, which is the acquisition, projection, and welding of power. Power is the way of the world and much of history is the drama of men, women, and nations in the pursuit for power, but shouldn't Western leaders be different? After all, our foundational story is Judeo-Christianity, and that story centers in large part around King David and his expressed desire to rule with love and justice. This divergence from our foundational story forces us to confront troubling questions. What presidents, prime ministers, senators, and members of parliament among others can we point to and say here is a man or woman who governs with love and justice? Western nations have thousands of men and women who participate in some form of governance yet we strain to name just one who possesses the virtues of love and justice. Is love and justice dead in Western civilization? And, if they are dead, can we assign the cause of death, and the date of their passing? We can do both. Love and justice died in Western civilization on December 26, 1914, the day after Christmas, and their cause of death is told in a single of work of art. This art is located a short distance outside of Vienna, Austria, and it has many stories to tell. Now, let's go to Vienna.

* * *

From 1st Century Jerusalem to Vienna present day.

Vienna is Europe's *la grande dame*. She is elegant, graceful, sophisticated, and the deep lines of age only add to her charm. That grace and beauty are visible in the city's Hofburg Palace and the nearby stables of the famous Spanish riding school. Just a short trolley ride away is the Schönbrunn Palace. Both are former residences of the Hapsburg Dynasty that ruled Europe for centuries. The splendor of St. Stephen's Cathedral fills the heart of the city, and a few blocks away, is the city's soul, the Vienna State Opera. We could spend days here, but the artwork we seek is located about fifteen miles southwest of downtown. As we wait for our hired car to arrive, we worry that our driver will not understand English, and be confused about where to take us. This fear is unfounded, because only a single word is needed to communicate our destination. The car pulls to the curb, we get in, and say, "Mayerling." He nods and enters the flow of traffic.

We're quickly out of the city, and after exiting the main highway, we're on a tranquil road passing through a lovely forest. Mayerling is a small village, but the village itself is not our destination. The work of art that is our stopping point resides in the convent that is adjacent the village. Typically, we think of European monasteries and convents as being hundreds, if not a thousand years old, and by that metric Mayerling's convent is an infant. The sisters of the Discalced Carmelites of Carmel St. Joseph have only been in Mayerling for about 130 years. The Carmelite order, however, dates back to the late 12th Century, and while it's exact origins are uncertain, it was likely established on Mt. Carmel at the time of the Crusades. Discalced means barefoot or wearing sandals like Jesus, and this humility defines their mission. The Carmelites are a contemplative order dedicated to prayer, worship, and the Eucharist, and the chapel in which the sisters at Mayerling worship is just up ahead.

It's not an imposing structure. A little over two stories in height, the chapel's Gothic entrance extends from the convent's pale yellow walls that are nestled among lower Austria's rolling hills and low mountains. The only sounds are the wind and hushed songs of birds in the surrounding forest. We slow our walk. This is a place of quietness, solitude, and serenity, and yet the irony is that just inside the chapel doors to the side is the art that tells the death story of love and justice.

We enter and as our eyes adjust to the dim light, we make our way to the side. Recessed into the wall before us is a statue of the Madonna. The statue sits in an eye-catching golden niche. Carved into the niche behind Mary is the top part of Jesus' cross. The statue of Mary is in the foreground. In her hands she holds the crown of thorns, and her gaze is upward and slightly to the left. Mary is posed as if only moments earlier Jesus had died, and a Roman soldier had just handed her the thorns that were pressed into his head. It is a touching scene that is tender with emotion, but garishly set into it is a bulging red heart on Mary's breast and suspended above her heart is a dagger, whose tip is ready to strike.

Of course, the scene depicted is not biblical. The artist was using his creative license to shock the viewer, and the shock is meant to convey the wrenching pain that Mary felt watching her son die on the cross. The interpretation is straightforward. However, the back stories associated with the Madonna and dagger statue converge to an interpretation that the artist could never have imagined. The back stories are like Russian nesting dolls, where the smallest story fits inside a slightly larger story and so on until everything is told. When we step back and look at the totality of these nested stories, a new interpretation emerges: the dagger pointed at the Madonna's heart, not only represents Mary's anguish at the death of her son, but Western civilization's pain at the death of love and justice that happened on December 26, 1914. Now, let's begin the stories starting with the smallest one, the person who commissioned this art.

The Empress consort of Austria, Queen consort of Hungary, Bohemia, Dalmatia, and Croatia, who was better known as Empress Elisabeth, commissioned the Madonna and dagger statue. If Empress Elisabeth had been born in the current age of social media, she would have been an international celebrity. Like Princess Diana, paparazzies would have stalked her. She would be on the cover of fashion magazines, and worldwide everyone would know her by her nickname, Sisi. But, she wasn't born in this age. In fact, she was born into a royal Bavarian family in 1837. Nobility comes with obligations, and Sisi at age sixteen was obliged to marry the 23-year old emperor of the Austro-Hungary Empire, Franz Joseph I, who was head of the Hapsburg Dynasty that had ruled vast regions of Europe for centuries.

The Empress Elisabeth was expected to fulfill her duties and carry-out her role as wife of the emperor according to the strict traditions of Vienna's Imperial Court. She did fulfill her primary duty which was to produce a male heir, but as for the rest? She broke the mold. Sisi was a thoroughly modern woman. She was obsessed with maintaining a slim figure, and most likely had an eating disorder. She fasted, dieted, and exercised until exhaustion to maintain her weight below 110 pounds, which was unhealthily thin for her 5'8" frame. Her waist was reported to be under 19 inches. To maintain such an obsessively slender figure, she converted a room in the palace into a gymnasium filled with 19th Century state of the art exercise equipment. A chinning bar, rings, medicine balls, and Indian clubs were among the equipment she used, and these exercises were supplemented with hours of walking and horseback riding. A strikingly beautiful woman, she was attentive to her appearance especially her long dark hair that fell to her ankles. Her hair alone required two hours daily to maintain, and she used all sorts of creams and odd regimens such placing thin strips of raw veal on her face to keep her skin moist and wrinkle-free. Of course, modern celebrities have a cause, and Sisi was no different. She insisted on more recognition for Hungary within the empire, and her insistency advanced the Austro-Hungarian Compromise of 1867 that gave Hungary its first prime minister.

Sisi also shared one additional characteristic of today's international elites. Her marriage and family relationships were convoluted and strained, and she was rumored to be having an affair with George "Bay" Middleton, a dashing English aristocrat. As the decades passed, Sisi took to traveling to escape palace life and her choice of transportation was the royal yacht. She sailed the Mediterranean Sea, and even built a residence for herself on the Greek isle of Corfu. But, Sisi's travels are more aptly described as restless wandering. She had a glass observation booth constructed on the deck of the royal yacht, and during voyages, she often sat alone in the booth for hours on end. She was especially fond of watching storms from its safety, which seemed to have an osmotic effect on her. In osmosis, the small drop of water is drawn to and fuses with the larger, and the magnitude of dark clouds hovering above a churning and chaotic sea seemed to pull the chaos from Sisi's soul into the larger storm before her, providing at least momentary relief from her cares. Her restless journeys, however, would lead to her undoing.

Sisi often traveled incognito, and at age 60, she was in Geneva, Switzerland, under an assumed named. The press, however, found her out and reported that Empress Elisabeth was staying at the Hôtel Beau-Rivage. Her security deal warned her of possible assassination attempts, but on Saturday, September 19, 1898, she ignored those warnings and walked along the shore of Lake Geneva with only her lady-in-waiting in attendance. This was the opening that a 25-year old Italian anarchist needed. He stalked the women as they strolled the lake, and when the opportunity presented itself, he approached the empress. Appearing to stumble, he bumped into her and struck, plunging a needle-like dagger into her chest.

The blade was so thin and sharp that at first even Elisabeth was unware of the extent of her wound. But, she soon collapsed and was carried on a stretcher back to her hotel room, where she died. The autopsy revealed that the sac surrounding her heart, the pericardium, had been pierced, just like the dagger pointed at the Madonna's heart in Mayerling. Soon, theories comparing the Madonna and dagger statute to the empress' death begin to swirl. In commissioning, the strange art had she unknowingly predicted the manner of her death? The remarkable similarly between the faces of the Madonna and the beautiful Elisabeth fueled the speculation. Continuing to today, many think that Sisi knew how she would die. Sisi's story is dramatic and tragic, but it is the smallest of our nested stories, and now we move to the second story in our quest to learn how love and justice died in Western civilization the day after Christmas in 1914.

Being slightly larger, our second story involves not only the statue, but Mayerling itself. The reverence and solemnity of the discalced Carmelite sisters as they move about their daily duties of the Divine Office is as far from Mayerling's previous activities as heaven is from hell. The Divine Office is a liturgy of scripture reading, recitation of prayers and worship, a time for personal private prayer, and most importantly celebration of the Eucharist. The Divine Office extends from midnight to midnight and its purpose is to sanctify each day to Our Lord. But, the activities that previously took place in Mayerling were much different. It was a hunting lodge, a get-a-away, hide-away kind of place acquired in 1886 by Crown Prince Rudolf of Austria, heir apparent to the Hapsburg Dynasty and the only son of Emperor Franz Joseph and Empress Elisabeth.

On the evening of January 29, 1889, Franz Joseph and Empress Elisabeth hosted a family dinner party. Rudolf, who was 30-years old, his wife, Stephanie, who was a princess in the royal house of Belgium, and their young daughter, Elisabeth, all dined together. Rather early in the evening, Crown Prince Rudolf said he wasn't feeling well and excused himself. Further, he said he had an early morning hunt to attend at Mayerling, and he wanted to be rested for it. Princess Stephanie was undoubtedly suspicious. Rumors of Rudolf's affair with the 17-year old Baroness Mary von Vetsera were the talk of the Imperial Court, and she suspected that her husband's early departure was for a rendezvous at Mayerling with his teenage lover. Franz Joseph and Empress Elisabeth had also heard the rumors, but as the servants cleared the dinner table and the family retired for the evening, they never expected the news they would receive in the morning.

Empress Elisabeth was the first in the royal family to hear the news. She was in the palace, taking her Greek lesson and was irritated at the knock on her door. Soon, however, she was weeping uncontrollably. She was told that earlier that morning, Loschek, the crown prince's valet, knocked on Rudolf's bedroom door at Mayerling, but the prince did not answer. Soon, the valet was pounding on the door, but still no response. Finally, Loschek smashed a door panel, reached in, unlocked the door, and entered. Rudolf was found sitting on the floor slumped against the side of the bed. His lover, Mary, lay on the bed. Both were dead of gunshot wounds. Rigor mortis had set in on Mary, but not Rudolf, suggesting that he had killed her and then hours later turned the gun on himself.

As the family mourned, the Imperial Court kicked into high gear. Stories that the crown prince had suffered an aortic aneurism were circulated, but as reporters descended on Mayerling, the true story crept out. As word of a possible murder-suicide spread, the royal family became concerned that the Roman Catholic Church would prohibit a church funeral and burial. After some careful diplomatic work, the Vatican issued a special dispensation asserting that Rudolf had been in a state of "mental imbalance," and with the dispensation came the approval for him to receive a church burial. Stories, rumors, and half-truths still swirled, and to stem this flood of sensationalism, Franz Joseph quickly donated the hunting lodge hide-away to the Carmelite sisters, who established the convent. Today, the chapel's altar rests of the location of Rudolf's bedroom, and the Madonna and dagger statue? Perhaps, it does represent Empress Elisabeth – Austria's beloved Sisi – and the dagger piercing her heart is the shocking death of her son. After the Mayerling incident, her wanderings began in earnest and eventually took her to Geneva, where her life tragically ended.

The smallest two nested stories are now told, and now we move to the larger third story that involves the empire itself.

Crown Prince Rudolf was Franz Joseph's only son. Without a male heir to succeed him to the Hapsburg throne, Franz Joseph's younger brother, the Archduke Karl Ludwig became the heir apparent. The archduke, however, died seven years later in 1896, and the title of heir apparent passed to his son, Archduke Franz Ferdinand. With the characters identified, now the story begins.

On Sunday, June 28, 1914, Archduke Franz Ferdinand, the second most important man in the empire, and his wife, Sophie, were in Sarajevo, Bosnia to inspect troops, which is seemingly an unimportant event for such an important man. Despite being the next in line as emperor, this royal couple was shunned at the Imperial Court in Vienna. Sophie, a Czech national, was from an aristocratic family, but her family was not of high enough rank to marry the heir apparent to the Hapsburg Dynasty. Therefore, before permitting the marriage, Emperor Franz Joseph, who refused to attend the wedding ceremony, required the archduke to renounce any claims or titles that would normally be bestowed to his wife as empress consort. Given this atmosphere, Franz Ferdinand and Sophie, who was pregnant, welcomed being away from Vienna, even for a troop inspection in Sarajevo. However, there would be no pomp and circumstance on this day. This Sunday would prove to be a fateful day not only for the Hapsburg Dynasty, but for Western civilization and the world. [35]

It was a clear summer morning in Sarajevo, and seemingly a peaceful Sabbath day, as Franz Ferdinand and Sophie's motorcade sped along Sarajevo's Appel Quay motorway on their way to the town hall. Then, the attack happened. A bomb was thrown at their open-topped car. It missed, bouncing off the folded convertible cover at the rear. The bomb fell onto the street and then detonated underneath the following car. The car was heavily damaged and two of the archduke's men were injured along with several bystanders. But, the royal couple, while shaken, were unscathed. Panicked, the archduke's driver accelerated and raced to the town hall.

Arriving at the town and trying to remain calm, the archduke attempted to keep to the itinerary. Sarajevo's mayor made a welcoming speech, which was ironic given that the visiting royal couple had just barely escaped assassination. The archduke then made a short address. When the formalities were done, the archduke and Sophie insisted on being taken to the hospital to see the members of their party who had been injured. Their cars were summoned, and the safest route to the hospital was hastily planned by security forces. But, amid the confusion and stress, no one bothered to tell the drivers that a new route, which was not the most direct, to the hospital had been chosen. The archduke was in the third vehicle of the motorcade, and when the two lead cars made a wrong turn onto a side street, the archduke's car followed. The governor, who was riding with the royal couple, immediately ordered the driver to stop. He did and when the driver reversed the car, it stalled.

Terrorists groups, Serbia's Black Hand working in conjunction with Young Bosnia, were behind the earlier bombing. While that attempt had failed to kill their target, they had not given up. Assassins were stationed along routes likely to be traveled by the archduke, and just steps from the archduke and Sophie's stalled car was a gunman. The archduke and his wife were exposed; totally vulnerable. The assassin raced into the street and as he jumped on the car's running board, he pulled the pistol given to him by the Black Hand. It all happened so fast there was no chance to react. He fired, striking the archduke in the neck. He fired a second time, hitting Sophie in the abdomen. The car raced to the governor's residence, where it was thought they could get medical attention. Sophie and her unborn child died in route and Franz Ferdinand soon after arriving at the residence.

When the tragic news reached the Hofburg Palace in Vienna, the 84-year old Emperor Franz Joseph's fury was unbroken by grief. He never really cared for the archduke or his wife, whom he considered a commoner. But, this assassination! It was an affront to Austria! The fingerprints of Serbia's Black Hand were all over the unsuccessful bombing and subsequent murder of the archduke, Sophie, and her unborn child. The emperor vowed that the conspirators would be brought to justice, and Serbians would be taught a lesson they would never forget. A list of twenty-five demands was quickly drafted. Serbia must cease all anti-Austrian propaganda, and allow Vienna to conduct a full investigation into the archduke's murder, were among the demands. Serbia accepted everything on the list except for one item, but this wasn't enough. With Germany's support, Franz Joseph mobilized the army and prepared an invasion force. From St. Petersburg, Russia, Tsar Nicholas II observed the rising tensions in the Balkans. Russia was not going to sit idly by and watch Serbia be crushed. The tsar pledged to defend Serbia, and with this action, the drums of war began to beat in Europe's capitals. On July 28, 1914, exactly one month after the assassination, Austria invaded, and all of Europe was on the eve of war.

Gazing at the Madonna and the dagger, we see what the nested stories have wrought. She represents not only Empress Elisabeth and the royal family, but all of Europe for a dagger was now poised and ready to strike at the heart of Western civilization. Europa herself was now threatened. How could this happen? How could Christian nation's whose leaders and citizens worship the same Savior, read the same scriptures, and receive the same baptism think that marshalling all their nations' might to kill the sons of another nation was a good idea? Our next nested story tells the tale, and being fourth and larger, this story begins by understanding the mindset of the time. Our story begins with La Belle Époque (The Good Times) that Europe had enjoyed for decades.

We have such a romanticized view of late 19th and early 20th Century Europe. We think that everyone in France had an easel, canvas, and oil paints in one hand and a loaf of French bread in the other. And, when they weren't dabbing little circles of paint on canvases in the new Impressionist style, we imagine they lounged in Parisian salons, nibbling on fresh gossip, while sipping fine wine. We have much the same notion about Britain thinking that everyone was like Lord Grantham and Head Butler Carson of the TV series Downton Abbey. They lived their lives in a small world and personal struggles were neatly resolved within a supportive tranquil village. It is true that La Belle Époque was a period of mostly peace and rising prosperity. And, of course it was a time of marvelous inventions – the airplane, telephone, electric lights, silent motion pictures, and mass production of automobiles. All these radically changed life. As for peace, the Napoleonic Wars were the last big conflict on the continent, and those had ended a century earlier. So what did happen? How was La Belle Époque broken? Historian Paul Ham in his book, <u>1913, The Eve of War</u>, said it all started with Europe's rulers. He wrote:

Far from shocking the rulers of Europe, the war that erupted in August 1914 was widely anticipated, rigorously rehearsed, immensely resourced and meticulously planned. By 1913, the leaders, if not the led, were anticipating and planning a major continental war, and to some extent those plans were so entrenched as to become self-fulfilling.[36]

Europe in the summer of 1914 was very much like the giant factories of that era. We've all seen grainy black and white photos of unsmiling men standing on factory floors adjacent to massive pulleys, belts, and flywheels. The machinery starts slowly, but once the pulleys, belts, and flywheels start spinning, they are near impossible to stop. In pre-war Europe, the factory machinery were the treaties and military alliances made by each nations' leaders. Germany, Austro-Hungary, and Italy were bound in the Triple Alliance, and Great Britain, France, and Russia were equally committed in the Triple Entente. The energy to run these machines was the patriotic fervor of a people who had not known a significant war in one hundred years. Add ignorance of the consequences of all-out war in modern industrialized nations to this mix, and the stage was set. All that was needed was the pull of a lever to get the machinery of war rolling.

When Austria invaded Serbia, the lever was pulled. The machinery started up slowly, but soon the factory was humming and churning out its product – death and destruction. Europe was quickly engulfed in the Great War, as it was called, and this war, like the dagger pointed at the Madonna, was a sharp blade into the heart of Western civilization. Caesar, the Roman emperor, crafted the blade that pierced the Madonna's heart, leaders of Europe's Christian nations who desired the will to power more than they desired the will of God, forged the weapons that stabbed the heart of Western civilization. With war underway, we now begin our fifth and final nested story. It's hard to imagine what story could be bigger than global war, but this story is larger because it involves heaven itself. This final story begins with Advent 1914.

For two thousand years, Western civilization has celebrated the coming of Christ. Every aspect of society is involved. We sing carols, and display the Nativity in our homes. Our children are Mary and Joseph, the shepherds, and Wise Men in school and church plays. Across the West, Christmas Day begins in church sanctuaries with midnight communion. All this is sacred, and of course there is the secular – gift wrapped presents, lighted trees, excited children. Both the sacred and the secular fills our hearts with wonder, warms our homes, and brings goodwill. It's who we are and that includes men in trenches whose patriotic duty is war.

By Advent 1914, the men in trenches had been at war for four long months. The no-man's land between the lines was littered with the dead. They could now see where this war was headed. It was a stalemate, and how to get more men, more ammunition, more artillery, more food, more of everything to the frontlines to breakthrough and win consumed the minds of generals. Therefore, what happened a few days before Christmas caught the makers of war in Europe's capitals by total surprise, but it shouldn't have. The men in trenches were merely answering the call of who they were. From the trenches, they began singing Christmas carols. Across the no-man's land, they shouted Christmas greetings to one another. Soon, they were out of their trenches, shaking hands and decorating whatever green tree or bush that was still alive. They exchanged small gifts and swapped stories of home – the wife who was waiting, the parents who missed their son, the girlfriend they intended to marry. Soccer games were played. You see, the men in trenches believed the angels' message of peace on earth goodwill to men, but the war makers in London, Paris, Berlin, and Vienna did not. They were frightened that this sudden expression of peace and goodwill might not be controllable. Now, that the men in trenches knew the names and stories of the men in the other trenches, would they obey the command to kill? This outbreak of Advent love and justice had to be snuffed out! Otherwise, this war was over just when it was getting started.

From Europe's capitals, the orders raced down the chain of command. Get this war started again! Through patriotic appeals, bullying, intimidation, and threats, officers on both sides forced their men back into the trenches. The date was December 26, 1914, and that was the day that love and justice died in Western civilization. By Christmas 1915, the hearts of the men in trenches were scared; their spirits shattered. For a year, each side had tried to overpower the other in flanking moves until the battle line on the Western front extended from Switzerland to the North Sea. The men in the trenches never again heard the voices of Advent's angels. On Christmas day, they only heard the grim rattle of death. By the time the guns fells silent in 1918, sixteen and half million lay dead and total war casualties stood at 32 million.

It has been 107 years since men in trenches stopped a war. It was an act of faith – not to mention courage – for soldiers to put down their rifles, climb out of trenches, and sing Christmas carols with so-called enemies. Whether British, French, German, or Austrian, they all shared the same Judeo-Christian foundational story. It is the story of the Lord God, who desires love and justice. It is the story of Our Savior, who forgives and offers mercy and grace. It is the story of the Holy Spirit, who comes from the throne room of God and fills our hearts with the knowledge of God. Most important to the men in trenches, it is the story of Christ, who conquered death. This is the power that stopped a war. It is the power of God, living in the hearts of common people. But, men can reject God. That is a right that he has granted humanity and in 1914 Europe's leaders exercised this right, not just for themselves, but for all of Western civilization. The consequences of their decision is staggering and remains with us today.

But, that story will have to wait. The chapel is closing. We'll return to Mayerling early tomorrow morning to resume the story, and to learn a deep truth that resides within Mayerling's walls. Before leaving, we take one last glance at the statue. This Madonna has many faces. She is Mary. She is Empress Elisabeth. She is the Hapsburg royal family. She is Europa and she is love and justice of which David sang. All her nested stories are told. But, we must keep in mind that the Madonna and dagger statue depicts Mary on Friday, the day of Jesus' death. Sunday and Christ's resurrection awaits. We'll hear that story and more when we return to Mayerling tomorrow.

Chapter 13:
Love & Justice, Part II

A psalm of David

The Lord says to my lord:
"Sit at my right hand
until I make your enemies
a footstool for your feet." (Psalm 110:1)

The language of the Bible is divine. It is pleasing to the ear and nourishing to the soul. The words give wings to our hearts, flying us to heaven, where God tells us that he knows our name and that we are so much more than flesh and blood. The verse quoted above, however, does none of these things. In fact, it leaves us scratching our heads. God is telling someone to sit down, there's a footstool, and somehow enemies are around. It's confusing. Yet the New Testament quotes this verse from the Old Testament more than any other. Three of the four gospels have Jesus quoting this verse to the Pharisees in the Temple in Jerusalem; see Matthew 22:44-45; Mark 12:36-37; Luke 20:42-44. Peter on the Day of Pentecost cited this verse in his sermon, proclaiming Jesus' resurrection and the coming of the Holy Spirit. (Acts 2:34-35) The writer of Hebrews mentioned this verse in the first chapter of that book. (Hebrews 1:13) It could not be more plain – this is a very important verse! Yet, its meaning is veiled and cryptic.

Perhaps, God in his divine wisdom wants us to search for its meaning. Jesus tells us that the one who "seeks finds." (Luke 11:10) This suggests that the desire to search and what we learn in the search are themselves important to understanding the meaning of this verse. Therefore, let's begin our search, and it starts where we left off yesterday with the Madonna and dagger statute at Mayerling. Even though it's still early in the morning, let's go there now.

* * *

From 1st Century Jerusalem to Mayerling, Austria present day.

Though the hour is still early, the summer sun arrived at Mayerling well before us. The lush summer growth glistens with morning dew, and as we walk to the chapel, a sudden rush of wind momentarily sways the tops of trees. The coolness of the breeze refreshes us, and carries the song of the Carmelite sisters through the open chapel doors out into the garden. In the hush of early morning, we hear lovely voices singing in Spanish. Carmelite is a global order and hymns sung in different languages is not surprising. We listen carefully. Relying upon our rusty high school Spanish, we repeat the phrase. "Nada te turbe, nada te espante." Let nothing disturb you, let nothing frighten you. As the summer breeze refreshes our body, these words refresh our souls. God is in control, and we'll need to keep these words in mind as the Madonna reveals her last story to us, which is the consequences of the death of love and justice in Western civilization that happened on December 26, 1914.

Quietly, we slip inside the chapel so as not to disturb the sisters. Immediately, we turn toward the side where the statue stands silent watch. For 130 years, she has observed the comings and goings of European history from her golden niche. Yesterday, the Madonna revealed her many faces. She is of course Mary, but also Empress Elisabeth, the Hapsburg royal family, and the Greek goddess Europa, who represents Western civilization. Importantly, she represents David, who sang praise to God, who rules with love and justice. But, as we learned yesterday, Western rulers do not share David or God's desire for governing with love and justice. Their desire is power, and to extend their power, they started a global war that at the time was called The Great War, but now is known as World War I.

When peace, love, goodwill, and justice spontaneously broke out during Advent 1914, rulers in London, Paris, Berlin, and Vienna vigorously opposed what was happening. Men left their trenches to sing Christmas carols with their so-called enemy. They exchanged small gifts, talked of home, and played games. The men in trenches were answering the call of who they were. They were Christians. They believed that the Messiah, the Son of God, was born in Bethlehem. They believed the angels' Advent message of peace on earth goodwill toward men. The faith and courage of these men in trenches stopped a war. But in Europe's capitals of London, Paris, Berlin, and Vienna, the rulers were determined to get the war restarted.

They didn't have to. The war had been underway for four months, and they could see that it was a stalemate. So why not use this outbreak of peace as the starting point for a general truce and peace negotiations? Their egos would not allow it, because their desire for power was greater than their desire for God's love and justice. So they compelled the men to get back into their trenches, and then ordered the sons of their nations to resume killing the sons of other nations. With that order, the rulers plunged a dagger into the heart of Western civilization. Europa herself was stabbed, and from that moment, her heartbeat which is Judeo-Christianity stopped, and from her wound spilled the virtues of love and justice.

The death of love and justice in the West is like the death of a father or mother in a family. The individual is essential to the health and well-being of the family, but the family must carry-on so they rely upon their memory of the person to make decisions and move forward. "What would dad do in this situation?" they ask themselves. This works for a while, but time passes and new generations, who never knew mom or dad, eventually guide the family. This is precisely what has happened in the West. It has been 107 years since Western rulers ordered men back into the trenches and commanded them to resume killing. A new generation of Western rulers, who have never been told they are expected to govern with the virtues of love and justice, is in charge. Is it any wonder that the Western family is adrift, purposeless, valueless, and godless? We have no agreed upon moral framework upon which to make decisions, and increasingly, we live in a civilization where might does makes right, because there is no aspiration to govern with love and justice.

Ensuing from the death of love and justice is the entire 20th and now 21st Centuries' history of the world. You may think that this is gross exaggeration – one event in a war that happened around Christmas 1914 certainly could not possibly be responsible for all that has happened in the last 100 years. Well, it is. The death of virtues as important as love and justice are that consequential, and it can be proved. To prove it, we'll use a technique employed in the Bible. We'll use the "begats."

The Bible, particularly in the Old Testament but also the New, gives lengthy genealogies. In the King James version, "begat" is the verb showing one generation giving rise to the next, as in "Abraham begat Isaac." (Genesis 25:19) Typically, we skip over these passages thinking they're unimportant, but that's a mistake. The "begats" are a means of stepping back and assessing what has taken place over generations. Beginning with December 26, 1914, a list of 20th and 21st Centuries' "begats" is offered. This list is global, encompassing all the nations of earth. Therefore, our list of "begats" is subdivided into world regions, and when you've reached the end of this list, you will unreservedly conclude that the death of love and justice changed the world.

The "Begats" of Western Civilization

- December 26, 1914, men ordered back into trenches begat the continuation of World War I;
- The continuation of World War I begat Germany smuggling Lenin into Russia and the subsequent Marxist revolution that overthrew the tsar;
- The overthrow of the tsar begat the deaths of untold millions of Russians;
- The continuation of World War I begat over 16 million dead and total casualties of 32 million;
- This death and destruction begat punishing terms against Germany in the Treaty of Versailles that ended the war;
- The harsh terms of the treaty begat the rise of Hitler and Fascism in Germany;
- Fascism in Germany begat the Holocaust and World War II;
- World War II begat over 50 million deaths;
- Those deaths begat the Paris Peace Treaties of 1947 that ended the war;
- These treaties begat Soviet enslavement of Eastern Europe and the deaths of somewhere between 50 to 100 million people living under the communist regime of the Soviet Union, and begat NATO and the Cold War;
- The Cold War begat the collapse of Soviet communism;
- The collapse of Soviet communism begat the absence of an enemy for Western democracies to fight;
- The lack of an enemy to fight and lack of God's love and justice begat a civilization without a purpose, and in this moral and spiritual vacuum godless Marxist ideology spread throughout the West;

- The spread of Marxist ideology begat the destabilization of Western civilization, causing all Western men and women to wonder who we are, what do we believe, what is our purpose;
- The destabilization of Western civilization begat a house divided and it cannot stand. (Mark 3:25)

The "Begats" of Eastern Civilization

- December 26, 1914, men ordered back into trenches begat the continuation of World War I;
- The continuation of World War I begat Germany smuggling Lenin into Russia and the subsequent Marxist revolution that overthrew the tsar;
- The Marxist revolution in Russia begat Marxist revolutions across Asian nations – China, Korea, Vietnam, and Cambodia:
- The Marxist revolutions in these nations:
    - Begat the civil war in China resulting in untold millions dead;
    - Begat the Cultural Revolution in China resulting in additional millions dead;
    - Begat the Korean War resulting in five million dead;
    - Begat the Vietnam War resulting in two million dead;
    - Begat the genocide in Cambodia resulting in two million dead;
- The Marxist revolutions in Asia begat the current rising tensions between the West and Communist China.

The "Begats" of Middle Eastern and African Civilizations

- December 26, 1914, men ordered back into trenches begat the continuation of World War I;
- The continuation of World War I begat the caliph of the Ottoman Empire (Turkey) entering the war on the side of Germany;
- Turkey's entry into the war on the losing side begat the end of the caliphate and dissolution of the Ottoman Empire;
- Dissolution of the Ottoman Empire and loss of the caliphate begat Western involvement in the Middle East.
- Dissolution of the Ottoman Empire coupled with Western involvement among other factors begat Muslim extremism and terrorism; X
- Muslim extremism and terrorism begat the 9/11 attacks on America;
- The 9/11 attacks begat 20 years of Middle East wars that further destabilized America and the West and drained trillions of dollars from Western economies. X

This is quite a dreadful list of "begats!" It is impossible to say that none of this would have happened if in 1914 Western rulers had listened to the men in trenches, sought peace, and ended World War I quickly. But what we can say is that like dominos falling, continuing the war allowed all the begats to fall one after another. If the war had stopped in 1914, then in 1917 Germany's rulers would never have smuggled Lenin into Russia. The sole purpose of returning him to Russia from exile in Geneva was to start a revolution that would end Russia's war against Germany. And, it worked, but look at the cost. How many millions have suffered and died under the boot of godless Marxism? Therefore, to conclude that love and justice died on

December 26, 1914 is not an exaggeration. The question is: where do we go from here?

The answer is: back to the beginning; back to the moment that the men in trenches stopped hiding, crawled out of the muck and dirt, and stood as free men with enough faith and courage to sing a Christmas carol in the middle of war. In that moment, Europe's rulers made a consequential – actually a world changing – spiritual decision. They thought they were only making a tactical war decision. They surely looked at what was happening on the Western Front and thought, "A rebellion, an insubordination led by some unruly men, who were likely cowards, has broken the chain of command. Just get them back in the trenches and deal with them harshly, if you must, but just make sure this doesn't happen again." But, it wasn't the men in trenches, who were the rebels. It was the Western rulers themselves. They were rebelling against Christ's teaching in the Sermon on the Mount. They were rebelling against God's desire that rulers govern with love and justice. The consequences of their spiritual decision to rebel against God and continue a war that had stopped wrought the blood soaked history of the 20th Century.

All this took place in the early decades of the 20th Century. So, where are we today in the early decades of this century? The decision in 1914 to rebel against God and forego governing with love and justice has given rise to generations of rulers, who haven't the faintest notion of governing with the virtues of love and justice. In their ignorance, they have gone one step further in their rebellion against God. They have made the spiritual decision to destroy the image of God in both man and nature. By destroying the image of God in what we see, it renders moot the question of whether or not there is a God who cannot be seen. In the 21st Century, Western rulers have led us through the looking glass. We are on the other side of the mirror from the debate between Christians and atheists on the existence of God. That was last century's debate. On this side of the looking glass in this century, God is moot, inconsequential, and nothing more than a quaint notion of angry zealots hanging onto unscientific mumbo-jumbo. "Where is God?" they shout, mockingly. "We don't see him or the image of him anywhere!"

Of course, the actual rulers – the presidents, prime ministers, members of congress, and members of parliaments – don't publicly use these words. They want to win elections and a residue of the old faith still lingers at least in the hearts of older Westerners, who vote. However, other Western rulers such as billionaires, celebrities, and elites in universities, who do not hold elective office but do have inordinate power, openly mock God and gleefully ridicule Christians. And, look at the decisions this cabal of elected and non-elected rulers have made. The ideas and forces they have unleashed in our civilization can lead only to a single conclusion. They are willfully destroying the image of God in both man and nature. Proving this point is surprisingly easy. In the list below, the biblical understanding of the image of God in both man and nature that has guided Western civilization for 2,000 years is offered first. That ancient Judeo-Christian understanding is then followed by Western rulers' new concept of the nature of our existence.

God created man in his own image, in the image of God he created him; male and female he created them. (Genesis 1:27)

Western rulers say their citizens are created in the image they decree. That gender is whatever they say it is, and they say there are many genders. Further gender is fluid; males can be females, females can be males, and in between are a host of genders. Hence, the confusion of our time.

The Lord God said, "It is not good for the man to be alone. I will make a helper suitable for him. Then, the Lord God made...woman. *For this reason a man will leave his father and mother and be united to his wife and they will become one flesh.* (Genesis 2:18, 22, and 24)

Western rulers say that marriage is whatever they say it is. Further, women don't need men's help, and it's demeaning to think that women should help men. Hence, the loneliness of our time.

> *What is man that you are mindful of him,*
> *and the son of man that you care for him?*
> *⁵ Yet you have made him a little lower than the*
> *heavenly being*
> *and crowned him with glory and honor.*
> *⁶ You have given him dominion over the*
> *works of your hands;*
> *you have put all things under his feet.* (Psalm 8:4-6)

Western rulers say that humans are simply another organism occupying this planet. There is no hierarchy of creatures, nothing is special about humans. Humans are merely a species of animal. Hence, the violence of our time.

God blessed them and said to them, "Be fruitful and increase in number; work it [the garden and by extension all of nature] *and take care of it"* (Genesis 1:28 and 2:15)

Western rulers say humans should decrease in number, not increase. And human's aren't capable of caring for the planet; we're killing it. Western rulers tell us that the world will burn up in... (pick the year because it changes constantly). Hence, the depression of our time.

God blessed the seventh day and made it holy. (Genesis 2:3)

Western rulers say that nothing is holy. Hence, the depravity of our time. ✗

And the Lord God commanded the man, "You are free..." (Genesis 2:16)

Western rulers say you are not free. In fact you are not even an individual. You are merely a classification. You are black, brown, white, gay, straight, lesbian, transgender, victim, oppressor, privileged, disadvantaged, conservative, liberal, other-abled, old, young and list goes on and on. But, one thing you are not, say Western rulers, is an individual created in the image of God, because if you were, then you would be free with rights that are granted from God. Hence, the oppression of our time.

In this short list, we see that the basis of our civilization and our understanding of life and freedom are being perverted and unrecognizably changed. Western rulers are willfully undermining the ancient wisdom and truth that created Western civilization for the purpose of remaking our civilization in their image. For their image to prevail, the image of God in the hearts and minds of men, women, and particularly children must be destroyed. We see it every day and the above list could be much longer. Just as the men in trenches in 1914 were surrounded by enemies, we too are surrounded by enemies that our rulers have created and unleashed. Now, we are ready to understand David's psalm that says:

The Lord says to my lord:
"Sit at my right hand
until I make your enemies
a footstool for your feet." (Psalm 110:1)

This verse is significant and oft quoted in the New Testament, because it is the clearest and earliest prophetic statement about Jesus. King David lived more than 100 years before the major prophets of the Old Testament, who prophesied that the Messiah would come to Israel. Further, the major prophets said that the Messiah would be from David's lineage, the House of Judah, and that he would be called the Son of God. In this psalm, David, who is a powerful king, writes that God is directing someone who is King over even David to sit at his – God's – right hand until God, not only subdues all of this person's enemies, but humiliates them by making them an object of ridicule – a footstool – in God's throne room. That person at the right hand of God is Jesus Christ. Therefore, roughly 900 years before the birth of Christ, God through David's poetry is giving us a glimpse into heaven's throne room, where pre-incarnate Christ sits in the position of power next to the Lord God Almighty. The enemies of God are placed on notice – your defeat is eminent. When this verse is placed in context with the surrounding psalms, it is not only prophetic, but speaks deeply to our daily human existence.

Psalm 110 is actually the answer to a question that David asked in Psalm 101 which is the psalm that began our journey to Mayerling. Psalm 101 begins:

I will sing of your love and justice;
to you, Lord, I will sing praise. (Verse 1)

In the second verse, David makes a statement and then asks God a question:

I will be careful to lead a blameless life—
when will you come to me?

Psalm 110 answers that question and the interpretation is: I will come to you when the Messiah comes. In between the question and answer of Psalm 101 and 110 is a collection of eight psalms that are symmetrically arranged to capture the pathos and exhilaration of the human condition.

Psalms 102 and 109 are prayers of a person in deep distress. Psalm 102 cries:

My days are like the evening shadow;
I wither away like grass. (Verse 11)

In Psalm 109, the person praying is – to use modern terminology – about being canceled.

...people who are wicked and deceitful
have opened their mouths against me;
they have spoken against me with lying tongues.
[3] With words of hatred they surround me;
they attack me without cause. (Verses 2 and 3)

Psalms 103 and 108 leave this pain behind and praise God' for his great love. Psalms 104 and 107 celebrate the goodness of God's creation and his redemption. Psalms 105 and 106 recount God's mighty acts in Israel. Psalm 106 says:

Who can proclaim the mighty acts of the Lord
or fully declare his praise? (Verse 2)

These ten psalms capture humanity's drama and God's great and boundless love, and the story in these psalms ends with the prophesy of the Messiah, who will defeat humanity's greatest enemy, death. The beauty, pathos, grace, and love poured out in these psalms speaks to our hearts, even when surrounded by enemies such as today. These ten ancient psalms witness that Western rulers are liars. All of nature belongs to the Lord, we are created in his image, and he loves us dearly!

We look up again at the Madonna and dagger statue. Yes Mary, you are in pain, but it's only Friday. Sunday is coming and with it your Son's resurrection. Death, man's greatest enemy, is a footstool under the Messiah's feet. While this promise of ultimate victory awaits people of faith, Western Christians are surrounded by people given license by our rulers to dispute all the doctrines of our civilization's ancient faith. We must deal with them the same way as the men in trenches in 1914 dealt with Western rulers, who rebelled against God, rejected his love and justice, and waged war. In the middle of that war, they climbed out of their trenches and greeted their enemy with goodwill and together they sang carols. This act of Advent love terrified Western rulers. Likewise, in the middle of this war of our time, we will climb out of the muck and filth of the trenches dug by our Western rulers, and as free men and women, we will sing. Christmas carols fortified the hearts of the men in trenches in 1914, and today the words of the Carmelite hymn will strengthen our hearts and give us courage. "Nada te turbe, nada te espante." Let nothing disturb you, let nothing frighten you. Our Savior lives! When that day arrives and Western men and women of faith and courage sing these words, Western leaders, like those in 1914, will be terrified, because they will know that the power of their godless grip on Western men and women is at an end. On that day, love and justice will return to our civilization.

Our time at Mayerling is at an end. That such a tranquil and out-of-the-way place is the epicenter for Western civilization's violent 20th Century history is most astonishing. But, we must never forget what Mayerling is now. It is a place of prayer, reflection, worship, and communion with Christ, where every day is sanctified to Our Lord. It is a place where we are restored to who we can be, which is a unique person, who is loved by Christ and whose inmost being was knitted in the womb by the hand of God. (Psalm 139:13) When God sends the Holy Spirit to awaken Western sleepers, then all Western nations will once again share in the wisdom of God, and will daily experience the love of God. On that day, peace like the peace here at Mayerling will return to the nations of the West. A new La Belle Époque (the good times) awaits our civilization.

We step out of the chapel into bright sunshine. It is a gloriously beautiful day. Puffy white clouds lazily drift in a crystal blue sky. A sudden gust of wind bends the summer grass and rustles the boughs of nearby trees. We are reminded of the ancient psalmist, who tells us that God *makes the clouds his chariot and rides on the wings of the wind. He makes winds his messengers.* (Psalm 104: 3-4) So with yearning hearts, we tune our ears to the wind, and hear, "Nada te turbe, nada te espante." In reply, we whisper, "Our Savior lives!"

Chapter 14: Goodness and Knowledge

[3] *His* [Jesus Christ's] *divine power has given us everything we need for a godly life through our knowledge of him who called us by his own glory and goodness.* [4] *Through these he has given us his very great and precious promises, so that through them you may participate in the divine nature, having escaped the corruption in the world caused by evil desires.* [5] *For this very reason, make every effort to add to your faith goodness; and to goodness knowledge*.. (2 Peter 1:3-5)

Peter, the great apostle, wrote these words near the end of his life. Perhaps, only a year or two at most after writing 2 Peter, he was martyred by the order of Emperor Nero in 68 CE. During his life, Peter was an eyewitness to things that two millennia later remain intriguing, controversial, inspiring, hopeful, amazing, and of course, miraculous. The feeding of the five thousand, the storm that was calmed, Lazarus stepping out of the grave, the crucifixion, and the resurrection – this is just a short list of the things that Peter witnessed. Now at the end of his life, what were the most important things on his mind? In a letter to the early church, that today we call 2 Peter, he offered encouragement, guidance, and warnings.

The church that was roughly three decades old was suffering under Nero's persecution, and inside the church were false teachers and evil men, who "mouth empty, boastful words, and by appealing to the lustful desires of sinful human nature, they entice people who are just escaping from those who live in error." (2 Peter 2:18) It was an uncertain, dangerous, and frightening time, and Peter was worried that Christians, who had only very recently experienced the light of Christ and the Holy Spirit in their lives, would be tricked by false teachers and evil men into returning to the sinful ways of the world. He warned them writing:

> [19] *They* [false teachers and evil men] *promise them* [the early Christians] *freedom, while they themselves are slaves of depravity—for "people are slaves to whatever has mastered them."* [20] *If they have escaped the corruption of the world by knowing our Lord and Savior Jesus Christ and are again entangled in it and are overcome, they are worse off at the end than they were at the beginning.* (2 Peter 2:19)

Peter, no longer the young and impetuous disciple but now the seasoned and wise pastor, needed to protect his flock from the lies of false teachers. His counsel to them were the verses that opened this chapter. He told them that the starting point was faith – be strong in the faith – and to faith add goodness and knowledge. Goodness is a Christian's personal effort to emulate Christ's humility and demonstrate love, forbearance, forgiveness, kindness, and virtue. Knowledge is, not only knowing what you believe, but understanding that there is evil, corruption, and depravity in the world. Knowledge is also recognizing that if goodness retreats in the face of evil, then we all become "slaves of depravity."

Westerners today very much live in world where goodness is in full retreat, and a key reason that goodness is on the run is because we no longer believe that evil exists. This belief is truly astonishing! The 20th Century was the bloodiest and most inhumane in recorded history. Millions died in combat, millions more starved, and still millions more were executed in Marxist or fascist genocidal massacres. Yet, the generations alive today, who did not witness firsthand the tragedy of that century, do not see that only true evil could produce such suffering and death. A prevailing Western belief is that people are good, that was then and this is now, life is good and will continue to be so. Really? What if that is a lie told by false teachers and evil men, who "promise… freedom while they themselves are slaves of depravity?" And, what if these evil men seek to make slaves of you? To those who don't believe in evil, this must sound outlandish and so over the top!

The story told below will dispel such thinking and shake naïve, foolish, and self-absorbed Westerners to the core. Our story begins with a sermon that was preached 67 years ago. It was a different world back then. It was a world where sharp lines divided good from evil, right from wrong, and freedom from slavery, and it really mattered on which side of the line you stood. Evil was very real, and goodness stood in opposition to it. With the sermon as the starting point, we will journey through the 20th Century and reveal how the evil that gripped that century still stalks Western men and women today. And, as Peter warned, should we become entangled in this evil, we will be "worse off at the end than [we] were at the beginning." All you who believe people are good and that evil is a myth perpetuated by your grandmother take special note.

* * *

***From 1st Century Jerusalem to Washington, DC, 1954*[37]**

As the last notes sounded from the organ, and faded into the upper reaches of the sanctuary, Dr. George M. Docherty checked his sermon notes one last time. He knew it was an important sermon, but as he rose and walked to the pulpit, he could not have imagined the impact his words that day would have. He cleared his throat and began:

Let me tell what 'the American way of life' is. It is gardens with no fences to bar you from the neighborliness of your neighbor. It is the perfume of honeysuckle, and the sound of katydids in the warm night air of summer, when you go out in the garden, the children long ago asleep, and you feel the pulse and throb of nature around you. It is Negro spirituals and colonial architecture. It is Thanksgiving turkey and pumpkin pie. It is the sweep of broad rivers and the sea of wheat and grass. It is a view from the air of the conflux of muddy rivers and neat little excavations and columns of smoke that is the mighty Pittsburgh. It is the canyons of the skyscrapers in New York, and the sweep of Lakeshore Drive that is Chicago. It is the lonely, proud statue of Lee on Gettysburg field. It is schoolgirls wearing jeans and schoolboys riding enormous push bikes. It is color comics. It is the Sunday New York Times. It is sitting on the porch on a Sunday afternoon, after morning church, rocking in a creaking wicker chair. It is a lad and lass looking at you intently in the marriage service. It is sickness and a home empty, quieted, and stilled by grief. It is the sound of the bell at the railroad crossing, and children's laughter. It is a solitary bugler playing Taps, clear and long-noted, at Arlington. And, where did all this come from?

This was 1954 America as seen through the eyes of Scotsman, Dr. George Docherty, who was the pastor of the historic New York Avenue Presbyterian Church in Washington, D.C. The occasion was Lincoln Sunday which is an annual tribute to the 16th President, who worshiped at the church. Today, the Lincoln pew remains in the sanctuary, and traditionally, presidents attend the Lincoln Sunday service that takes place in February near the late president's birthday. On Sunday, February 7, 1954, President Eisenhower and his wife, Mamie, were in attendance and seated in the Lincoln pew.

The America painted by Dr. Docherty on that Sunday morning was a familiar one to the president. He was from Kansas, the heartland. Honeysuckle, katydids, the sea of wheat and grass, and a Sunday afternoon on a front porch were the things of his youth that Eisenhower carried to the U.S. Military Academy at West Point. These things of the heartland no doubt stayed with him as he rose through the ranks to become the general of the mightiest army that ever marched – the army that liberated Europe from fascism and death. For General Eisenhower, the thunder of canon and the chaos of battle were all too familiar, as was the "solitary bulger playing Taps" at Arlington National Cemetery. The America described by Docherty was one that the president certainly recognized. It was the America that he knew and loved. In this 1954 sermon, the preacher asked, "Where did all this come from?"

Sixty-seven years – roughly three generations – have passed since that Lincoln Sunday sermon. The America that so captivated Dr. Docherty, the Scotsman, no longer exists today. The obvious question – where did all this go? – relies upon contemporary mindsets to judge the recent past, and we are not unbiased judges. As 21st Century Americans, we bring our own knowledge of history, as well as our ignorance, and our own brand of "woke" morality to inform our opinion on the changing of America. Opinions will not only differ but will splinter into opposing camps that will argue over the rightness of their judgment, regarding the goodness or villainy of America's past. In this argument that grows more vicious and desperate by the year lies the penetrating truth about who we are as Americans.

The truth is this: today we face two great challenges. One is to understand the goodness of who we were, and the other is to know the evil of who we are becoming. These challenges are revealed by modern-day Americans inability to grasp Dr. Docherty's message. We can surely visualize images of white picket fences, hot dogs sizzling on a backyard grill, and the flag flapping in a gentle breeze, but what we cannot conceive of today is the goodness that breathed life into America. It was a goodness that like a cord bound together people, place, and destiny and tied them to the American heart. This holy cord of goodness is what Docherty saw in America, and it is what we are losing, and perhaps we've already lost. The consequence of this loss is an identity crisis. We no longer know who we are as a person or as a people.

America, however, is about overcoming challenges. The key to overcoming our crises of societal and personal identities is to answer the seminal question: what exactly was the holy cord of goodness that bound Docherty's America together and tightly secured it to his heart? Fortunately, we don't have to guess. Docherty provided the answer in his sermon. It was "under God." His Lincoln Sunday sermon resulted in those two words being added to the Pledge of Allegiance on Flag Day, June 14, 1954.

In his sermon, Docherty recalled his children returning home from school. He asked them what they did that day, and they replied that like each day it began with the pledge of allegiance to the flag. Being Scottish, he was unfamiliar with it, and he asked them to recite it. As he reflected upon the words, he said that "I came to a strange conclusion. There was something missing in this pledge, and that which was missing was the characteristic and definitive factor in the American way of life." The American way of life, he concluded, is defined by being "under God."

In Docherty's view, the American way of life was shaped by the "fundamental concepts of life [that] had been given to the world from Sinai, where the moral law was graven upon tablets of stone, symbolizing the universal application to all men," and the goodness of America "came from the New Testament" and "the words of Jesus of Nazareth, the living of Word of God for the world." He said that Lincoln clearly saw this connection too, and that it served as his inspiration in the Gettysburg Address, when he said, "that this nation under God shall have a new birth of freedom." In this profound phrase, Docherty said that Lincoln "was simply reminding the people of the basis upon which the nation won its freedom in its Declaration of Independence."

In 1954, the freedom of America and the West stood in stark contrast to the communist repression and slavery of the Soviet Union and her satellite states in Eastern Europe. Globally, communism was on the march. China was, as it is today, a communist nation. Southeast Asian governments were falling to communist insurgents. Cuba along with other Latin American nations were under attack. In 1956, two years after Docherty's sermon, Nikita Khrushchev, First Secretary of the Communist Party of the Soviet Union, told the West, "My vas pokhoronim!" ("We will bury you!") Nuclear weapons made his threat very real! This was the global reality in which Dr. Docherty's Lincoln Sunday sermon was set: the Cold War was in full swing.

The Cold War began at the conclusion of World War II and continued until 1989. The beginning of end happened when the Berlin Wall that separated democratic West Berlin from communist East Berlin was torn down. These decades of conflict are described in terms of democracy versus dictatorship, capitalism versus communism, and individual freedom versus collective slavery to the state. Dr. Docherty saw the Cold War as encompassing all these things, but he believed that the fundamental basis of the conflict was moral and spiritual. On this Lincoln Day, he said, "We face today, a theological war. It is not basically a conflict between two political philosophies – Thomas Jefferson's political democracy over against Lenin's communistic state. It is a fight for the freedom of the human personality. It is not simply man's inhumanity to man. It is Armageddon, a battle of the gods. It is the view of man as it comes down to us from Judeo-Christian civilization in mortal combat against modern secularized, godless humanity."

Having witnessed two world wars, Dr. Docherty on that 1954 Sunday had no idea how this theological war would end. Today, having the benefit of 67 years of hindsight, we know that that one after another communist states in the early 1990's collapsed. The prevailing thinking was, and is: America and the West won the Cold War. This is true in the sense that the communist form of government in Russia and the nations of Eastern Europe no longer exist. However, the theological war, the moral and spiritual war, and "the fight for the freedom of the human personality" that Docherty saw never ended.

The reason this moral and spiritual war continues to be fought is because the communist ideal of a science-based, modern, secularized, godless society was never defeated. Fascism was defeated. At the end of World War II, Nazi Germany's war machine was a pile of rubble. From the rubble emerged images and stories that shocked the civilized world. Death camps, barbaric medical experimentation, and genocide revealed the true *Geist*, i.e., spirit, of a godless, science-based society. It was slavery, brutality, and death. Therefore, the world turned away from Nazi Fascism in horror, and fascist ideology was repudiated. A world away, Imperial Japan was defeated too. Like Nazi Germany, in defeat, the true nature of the Empire of the Rising Sun was shown to the world. It was death camps, torture, rape, slavery, and genocide, and the civilized world was appalled by godless, nationalistic, racial imperialism.

Communist ideology, however, was never similarly defeated, exposed, and repudiated. The Cold War thankfully never sparked into a "hot war." Moscow was never invaded. Her archipelago of prison camps were never liberated by NATO troops, and the world never gazed in horror upon pictures of half-starved, hollowed-eyed men in rags staring blankly at the camera as they emerged from the camps. Certainly, Stalin and his henchmen killed millions – as did Mao in China – but the West never tried, convicted, and executed communists for war crimes and crimes against humanity, as was done with Nazis and Japanese imperialists.

The Nuremberg war crimes trial of Nazis, and the war crimes trial of Japanese imperialists, along with the confession by the emperor of Japan that he was not a god sealed the fate of these cruel and enslaving ideologies. But, this wasn't the fate of communism. Instead, communist ideology in Eastern Europe and Russia collapsed from its own burden of evil, godless inhumanity and economic devastation. Never repudiated, the ideology during the 1990's and early 21st Century morphed so that it was no longer primarily identified as an economic system. Communist ideology, like the Greek mythological serpent, Hydra, sprouted multiple heads.

State ownership of everything was recast as fairness. Class warfare was replaced by victims of white Judeo-Christian repression seeking equity. The communist necessity to devalue the individual and human life was cloaked, and in its place, the sustainability and life of the planet was elevated over the life and property of the individual. The cruelty of a worldview that values sustainability of the planet over the sustainability of human life on that planet was so successfully concealed that today the lives of new born infants are weighed on perverse scales of godless justice to determine whether they live or die. While these disguises are clever, one deception in particular trumps them all: the godless secularized brutality of the state was rehabilitated and said to be more compassionate than the Judeo-Christian God, who was redefined as a god of hate. This was a master stroke! Now disguised with new terminology and so-called new progressive thinking, the evil so-called science-based ideology slipped into America and all the nations of the West.

Undefeated, the new multi-headed communist ideology entered Western civilization like a stealthy virus. Viruses hijack their host's normal functions. Outwardly, everything looks the same, but the foreign substance twists what's normal, creating a new normal that is in fact quite abnormal. This is exactly what disguised godless, secularized, science-based ideology has done to America and the West. For millennia, the prevailing normal was Judeo-Christianity. Our institutions, rights, freedoms, self-identity, and national creeds were rooted in the faith. To use Dr. Docherty's words, we were under God. But with the infection, all this was set to change, and riding the tide of that change was destruction of our goodness as a person, and the unraveling of the holy cord of goodness that binds us together as a people.

The goodness of our identities had to be the first casualty in this fight. Otherwise, we would resist, because American and Western identities, like our institutions, rights, and freedoms, are defined by Judeo-Christian beliefs. At the center of the deepest innermost sanctum of our personality is the understanding that we are created in the image of God. We see ourselves and others as sacred, spiritual creatures created, not evolved, and thus bearing God's imprint. We believe as scripture says that "He has also set eternity in the human heart." (Ecclesiastes 3:11) This view of life is the starting point for two millennia of Western civilization, but what keeps our civilization so alive and so vibrant is that it is infused with the knowledge that we have a Redeemer, Jesus Christ, and that God is active in the present world through the Holy Spirit. This is who we were. This is what Docherty understood as the goodness of America, and for the godless virus to be successful, our knowledge of God had to be erased and replaced with a twisted and corrupted image of God. It had to be so, because if our knowledge of God was simply absent, we would look for

Our Creator and find him, because the Bible tells us that "he is not far from any one of us." (Acts 17:27) Without knowledge of God, we had no defense in what Docherty called "the fight for the freedom of the human personality," and the destruction of our goodness as a person and people was underway.

The destruction came slowly, because memories, of the true inhumane, oppressive nature of godless secularized ideologies were horrifically vivid during the Cold War. Walls, guards, people shot trying to escape, depravation, prison camps – as long as these memories and more were alive, Americans could see through the disguise, and our human personality was protected. However, memories fade with the passing of generations, and without fresh examples exposing life in a godless secularized society, the memory defense erodes. But, there is more afoot here than memory loss. There is willful deceit.

In the late 20th Century, America's universities, i.e., the Academy, decided not to retell the history of Western civilization, and as a result the three generations, who were not alive, at the time of Dr. Docherty's sermon, lack the foundational information, i.e., the knowledge, to fully assess the theological, moral, and spiritual threat posed by a godless secularized society. Nor can these generations fully appreciate the role of Judeo-Christianity as the underpinning of American freedom. Such a lack of appreciation is truly astonishing since both Jefferson in the Declaration of Independence and Lincoln in the Gettysburg Address clearly acknowledged that our freedom is under God. Further, these three generations cannot fully comprehend that the standard of justice applied in the war crimes trials convened at the end of World War II were wholly Judeo-Christian! Such ignorance is excusable, because the blame must be laid squarely on the doorstep of the Academy.

As the first and most prominent victim of the godless, secularized disease, the Academy could not abide teaching the history of a civilization shaped by the God and Savior, who is at the heart of Judeo-Christianity. The Academy abandoned Westerners, and the goodness of America began to fade. With time, a collective amnesia afflicted America. Something was missing, something had changed. We didn't know what is was, but there was an absence, a hole in our soul, and the Academy rushed to fill it. Instead of resuming the centuries old practice of presenting a holistic telling of history, the Academy adopted one of failed communism's most effective disguises. It created a fragmented retelling of history told from the perspective of victims, i.e., a class or group who were oppressed and harmed under the Judeo-Christian ethic that is Western Civilization.

Today, the educated class of America, which is quite large, understand Western civilization not as an ancient and good society, whose history, institutions, justice system, liberties, and charities were birthed in biblical scripture. Rather the educated class understand America's history, to be a mosaic of victims oppressed by Judeo-Christianity and the church. If this confusion could be corrected by a factual retelling of our history, then the remedy is simple enough. Blow the dust off textbooks. Unleash truthful scholars and empower honest teachers. Then the first of our great challenges – knowing who we are as a people – could be overcome. But, it's not that easy. We have lost something much more deep and profound than America's history. In losing our knowledge of God, we lost awareness of his holy cord of goodness that binds together person, place, people, and story, and ties them to the heart. We have lost transcendent love.

In 1954, Dr. Docherty intuitively understood the nature of the holy cord of goodness, because transcendent love runs throughout his description of America. What is America he asked and answered, "It is a lad and lass looking at you intently in the marriage service. It is sickness and a home empty, quieted, and stilled by grief. It is the sound of the bell at the railroad crossing, and children's laughter. It is a solitary bugler playing Taps, clear and long-noted, at Arlington." These are images of lives lived, lives that passed, and an eternity that received them, as expressed by railroad tracks whose origin and terminus lie beyond the horizon. Most importantly, these are images of love – a bride and groom on the doorstep of life together, grief over loss of a loved one, and fraternal love for a fallen brother or sister. Such love is transcendent. It is holy. It is good. It is a love that comes from a shared history, a shared story, and a shared faith, but this holy love does not live in the past. It very much lives in the present, and because it is alive and vigorous, it runs toward a future with hope. However, the true home of holy love, and where it achieves fullest expression is beyond the future, which is eternity, the dwelling place of God.

Transcendent love is the holy cord of goodness that is spun in God's throne room. Through time and space, it binds home to heart and places both under God. For four centuries from Jamestown Colony to Dr. Docherty's sermon and beyond, it lassoed the hearts and minds of Americans and made us who we are. It gave birth to America and American ideals of freedom, justice, mercy, and charity. This is the goodness that Dr. Docherty saw. It was an America bound by the holy cord to eternity and the God, who dwells there.

This imagery does not imply perfection. Nor is it a statement that seeks to minimize or diminish past injustices or wrongs. No society has ever been perfect! However, a society under God has a moral map given to us by Judeo-Christianity, e.g., what Dr. Docherty called the "fundamental concepts of life [that] had been given to the world from Sinai," and "the words of Jesus of Nazareth, the living of Word of God for the world." Following this moral map is in fact the very reason that America and other Western nations have corrected grievous injustices.

The abolitionist movement to end African slavery originated in and was carried forward by churches. The gospel message of Christ's love and redemption, and the equality of all peoples in the eyes of God could not be reconciled with ownership and bondage of fellow human beings. William Wilberforce (1780-1825) in England believed that God had given him the mission to end Great Britain's involvement in the African slave trade. Through his effort, parliament passed the Slavery Abolition Act in 1833. In the U.S., Sojourner Truth (1797-1883) who was born a slave and later emancipated, believed it was God's will that she work for the abolition of slavery. While African slavery endured for far too long, ultimately this sin was ended at the cost of over 600,000 lives in the Civil War. That a nation would accept such a staggering cost of life and its accompanying suffering only illustrates the strength of America's resolve to follow her moral map. A century later from the pulpit of churches, Dr. Martin Luther King called for the abolition of laws that discriminated on the basis of race. With eloquence and courage, he pricked the nation's conscience. Jim Crow laws endured for far too long, but ultimately, this sin too ended. Laws were changed.

Today, the Civil Rights Movement of the 1960's is characterized as social justice. Justice needs no – nor should it have – any qualifiers. Justice in all Western nations is correction of violations against civilization's moral and spiritual foundation, i.e., our Judeo-Christian moral map. In fact, the entire dreadful history of 20th Century wars and communist oppression during the Cold War was a substitution of justice by social justice. After all, what is Nazism, communism, and Japan's racial imperialism other than a nation's immoral social justice de jour? Given this history, it is truly astonishing that Western men and women are so confused and cannot see that all morals, all justice, all freedoms, all corrections of injustices originate from nations and peoples, who are – as Dr. Docherty said – under God. There is no such thing as social justice. There is only the will to power, and standing in opposition to it is justice. And, justice is desired and pursued by a people following the moral map and bound together by holy love. Such people strive toward a new birth of freedom under God just as President Lincoln said. Free people under God are moral, hopeful, optimistic, and resilient, because they live in the shadow of eternity.

Today, however, three generations of Americans believe we live in the shadow of death with many imagining that human life will survive only for a dozen years more. Such a breathtakingly grim idea is possible because of what we've lost. We no longer believe that we are created in the image of God, who has reserved a place for us in heaven. We no longer believe that God is love or that a Savior redeems us for eternity. We no longer believe that we are stewards of Creation, but rather we see ourselves as agents of death to our planet that is hung in a dark and godless universe. Therefore, we stand outside church doors believing there is nothing inside worth believing, and our concept of God, who dwells in eternity, is as empty as church pews. The Academy abandoned Westerners, but Westerners abandoned the church. Lacking faith, we have no idea of who we are as a person, and lacking faith, we cannot fully appreciate the divine richness of our history; thus we cannot know who we are as a people. We are depraved amnesiacs who actually believe that a godless secularized society can achieve greatness, when 100 years of evidence and two world wars have vividly shown, it only produces suffering and death.

Americans are like Romans at the beginning of the Dark Ages. Within decades after the total collapse of Rome vast knowledge was lost. Romans could see the aqueducts, the massive buildings, elaborate public baths, and the Coliseum, but they had no idea how they were built. Today, millions of Americans live within the freedoms, accomplishments, and achievements of our civilization and have no idea how they were built. The Dark Ages, however, were ended by the Renaissance, a rebirth. Likewise, our current darkness will be ended by a rebirth of faith. But, we look around us in America, Europe, and in all Western nations and we see scant evidence for a rebirth of faith.

Just as dark gray skies and the hard frosty ground of winter hides the germination of seedlings readying for spring, perhaps that's where the America is today. As we wait, let us have faith and pray that the dark winter of false teachers and evil doers is coming to an end, and let us follow Peter's instruction to the early church by making "every effort to add to your faith goodness, and to goodness knowledge." Once again America will be "under God."

Chapter 15:
Worship and Fellowship

[1] As the deer pants for streams of water,
so my soul pants for you, my God.
[2] My soul thirsts for God, for the living God.
When can I go and meet with God? (Psalm 42:1-2)

These four lines penned by an ancient psalmist subtly reveals the quiet desperation of the human heart. He imagines a deer on the run. Perhaps the creature is being pursued by a hunter or a natural predator. Whatever the threat, the graceful creature relies upon speed, leaps, and camouflage to elude, hide, and stay alive. But in this race for life, he pants and thirsts. He must find water and rest, if only for a moment. In this frantic scene the psalmist stealthily replaces the deer with himself. "My soul thirsts for God, for the living God."

In this race of life, particularly in the modern world, we are on the run; sometimes pursued and sometimes the pursuer. We elude, hide, and stay alive. "It's a jungle out there," is a common Western expression. Like the deer, we can't run forever, hiding is tiring, and staying alive is not living; such is the quiet desperation of modern Westerners. Our souls thirst and need spiritual rest, if only for a moment. The psalmist identifies our spiritual thirst, telling us that his thirst is "for God, for the living God," and he asks the question, "When can I go and meet with God?" It wasn't a question of where, but when.

The psalmist believed the deer knew where to find water, and he believed he knew where to find and meet God, but today Western men and women do not believe we can find God let alone meet with him. We think the notion of meeting with God is foolishness. Yet our souls thirst, and we find nothing in the modern West that says, "Here is water, living water. Come and drink." Believing there is no "living water" (see John 4:10), the Western soul is not just thirsty, but parched and dry. Even while our souls grow more desperate, we believe there is no place where we can go to meet the Living God, and find refreshment and rest for our souls.

The ancient Hebrew psalmist would be baffled by our mindset. He knew where he could go and meet God. It was in the Temple in Jerusalem, and before the Temple was built, God dwelled in the Tabernacle of the Exodus which was a tent that moved with the Children of Israel as they journeyed through the Sinai. The scriptures tell us that the Tabernacle was also known as the "tent of meeting." (Exodus 40:2) Sacrifices and ceremonial cleansing at the entrance to the tent of meeting prepared priests to enter and meet God (see Exodus 38-40). What if the psalmist is right, and we, Westerners, are all wrong? What if there is a place where we can go and meet God? What if there are hints and signs all around us that God has prepared a tent of meeting for us to enter and quench our thirsty souls with his "living water?"

Let's just for a moment set aside our doubts, and take a trip in search of the tent of meeting. Our journey will begin on one of Paris' most wealthy and affluent boulevards. As the French say, "Allons-y!" (Let's go!)

* * *

From 1st Century Jerusalem to Paris present day

We arrive at Paris' Gare du Nord train station and take Metro Line #4. Our stop is the Saint Michel station. Climbing the stairs, we step out of the dimness of the underground station and make our way to a lovely boulevard. We are in Paris' Latin Quarter on the Left Bank, and we are standing on the Boulevard de Saint-Germain. It's a busy street, lined with swank shops, expensive restaurants, quiet cafes, and highly sought-after apartments. We're definitely in Paris' high-rent district, which is seemingly an unlikely place to find God's tent of meeting, but it's here. We just need to look for it. To our right is the Ile de Cité and Notre Dame Cathedral or what's left of it, since the devastating 2019 fire. But, Notre Dame is not our destination. We head in the opposite direction, walking along the boulevard. Resisting the urge to window shop, we navigate the crowded sidewalk and in a few short blocks we come to the remains of once grand and ancient buildings. Impressive stone walls still stand and littered among the walls are stones that fell centuries ago. These are the ruins of Roman baths that were built in the 3rd Century and are called *Les Thermes de Cluny*.

By the 3rd Century, Christianity had taken root in the Roman Empire. Churches established by the apostles and early converts were now more than one hundred years old. Despite persecution, new churches were being rapidly added. While this time period of the early church can teach us much about how and where we meet God, and how we prepare ourselves to worship and fellowship with him, these ancient Roman baths are not our destination. But, we are very close. Our stopping point is just next door at the Musée de Cluny.

The Musée de Cluny is a magnificent building, and one of the few remaining examples of medieval architecture in Paris. So, it's no surprise that the museum's collection consists of artifacts from the Middle Ages. The building itself dates from 1334, when it was constructed as a Parisian townhouse for visiting abbots from the Cluny Monastery located in Saône-et-Loire, which is a hundred or so miles southeast of Paris. As one of the wealthiest and most influential monasteries in Europe, Cluny, a Benedictine Order, required a townhouse or *Hôtel de Cluny*, as it was known, to accommodate the abbots and to remind Parisians of Cluny's importance. Founded in 910, Cluny prospered through the centuries, but the monastery was disbanded in 1790 during the French Revolution, and some fifty years later, the building became a museum in 1843. Today, the museum houses thousands of art and artifacts from the Middle Ages, and its most treasured work of art is the key to finding the tent of meeting.

As the museum's most prized possession, this art is housed in the building's lowest level, where light and humidity can be more easily controlled. To get to this special exhibit room, we walk through room after room of medieval artifacts, and the theme and inspiration for virtually all the displayed pieces is Christianity. Crucifixes of every description, ranging from fine and detailed craftsmanship to simple and crude, fill display cases. The same can be said for the carved wood altarpieces. Many are large, elaborate, and detailed while others are simple and unadorned. From chalices to communion plates to cross necklaces and rings, the influence of Christianity is unmistakable. One curious artifact, however, seems out of place. But, once we identify its purpose, we grasp the depth to which medieval life was filled with the Christian faith.

This piece is crudely made and looks as if it would have been a child's toy. It's a small wood carved donkey that's about the size of a cocker spaniel. The donkey stands on a platform with wheels and at one time a rope was fastened to its mouth like a bridle and rein. On the donkey's back is the carved figure of a bearded man, wearing a robe. Each Palm Sunday, a small village in medieval France would reenact Jesus' triumphal entry into Jerusalem by pulling the donkey and Jesus through the village streets to shouts of "Hosanna!" Through centuries of reenactments and teaching, the story of Christ sank deep into the marrow of the West. The story was also communicated through calendars, where planting and harvesting, pasturing and shearing, calving and foaling, and all the other things of farm life moved to the rhythm of days dedicated to saints. As flowing water over time smooths and shapes stones, the character of Western civilization was shaped by Christianity. It is who we were, and though we try, it is what we cannot escape. Judeo-Christianity is the core of the West's foundational story, but this still doesn't tell us about the tent of meeting. Therefore, let's now view the museum's most prized art and find answers.

Stepping into the exhibition room, we see several very large and richly woven tapestries suspended from the ceiling and displayed in a semi-circle. These are The Lady and the Unicorn tapestries. Six in total, the wool and silk panels were woven in Flanders around 1500. The background of each features exquisitely woven delicate flowers, which gives this style of tapestry its name, mille-fleurs (a thousand flowers). In the foreground of all six tapestries is a noble lady with a unicorn to her left and a lion on her right. Various other animals appear too. Monkeys, rabbits, dogs, and goats are some of the animals that are delightfully woven into each of the six scenes. On closer inspection, we notice in some panels that the unicorn and lion wear armor that bears a coat of arms. Likewise, the pennants display the same coat of arms. Sponsors of medieval and Renaissance art liked to insert themselves into the art they paid for, and this coat of arms belonged to the rich and powerful Le Viste family.

The key to interpreting the tapestries is what the lady is doing in each panel. In one she stands touching the unicorn's horn with one hand and holding the pennant in the other. In another panel, the lady is taking sweets from a dish held by a maidservant. In the third panel, the lady is making a wreath of flowers, and a monkey on a bench to her left has stolen one of the flowers and is smelling it. In the fourth, she is playing a small pipe organ, and in the fifth panel, the lady is seated and holding a mirror in her right hand that reflects the unicorn's face. The unicorn and lion appear in each panel watching as the lady illustrates the five senses: touch, taste, smell, hearing, and sight. The sixth tapestry is wider than the others and features a slightly different style. What the lady is doing in this tapestry transforms the art. These six panels are not merely a fanciful representation of the five senses. They are in fact, a deep and profound commentary on the human condition that provides unmistakable evidence that God has prepared a tent of meeting for us.

In the sixth tapestry, the lady stands in front of a tent with her maidservant to her left holding an open box. The lady has removed her necklace and is placing the jewels in the box. The tent behind her has an inscription above the door that reads *À mon seul désir* – My only desire.

What the artist had in mind by placing this inscription above the door is unknown. A common interpretation is that courtly love is the lady's only desire. In the Middle Ages, courtly love was the romance of chivalrous knights, bold adventures, and courageous deeds where the damsel is rescued by her love; her only love. But, this explanation doesn't fully consider the theme of the other panels and the fact that she's removing her jewels before entering the tent really doesn't support a courtly love interpretation. A fuller explanation is that the experiences of the senses, i.e., the sensual world, can be pleasing, delightful, and satisfying, but sensual pleasures do not satisfy the most important desire in life. This interpretation is reinforced in the sixth tapestry that finds the lady removing her necklace before entering the tent to fulfill her *À mon seul désir*. Her only desire is inside the tent. Outside the tent are the delights of the senses, the jewels of the world, the beauty of nature, and the spirit of curiosity and imagination. After all, who has ever seen a unicorn? Yet none of these satisfied the lady's *À mon seul désir;* only what was hidden inside the tent could meet that need.

A.W. Tozer, a noted 20th Century pastor and writer described this type of desire and its fulfillment as follows: *Before the Lord God made man upon the earth He first prepared for him by creating a world of useful and pleasant things for his sustenance and delight. In the Genesis account of the creation these are called simply "things." They were made for man's uses, but they were always meant to be external to the man and subservient to him. In the deep heart of man was a shrine where none but God was worthy to come. Within him was God; without a thousand gifts which God had showered upon him.* [38]

The shrine that Tozer is describing is the tent of meeting. It is our most inner sanctuary, our truest self, a place where only God is worthy to enter. When we meet God in the tent of meeting, our response is to worship him, who is Our Creator and Savior. Through fellowship with God, our thirsty souls drink living water, and our chief desire in life is met. At last, we know that we are loved.

Like the lady in the tapestry, before entering the tent, our jewels and things of this world are laid aside, and do not confuse laying aside with rejection. The jewels are merely placed in a box, and all the senses remain intact. They are all still there for use, enjoyment, and delight, but they are lesser than and subservient to the *À mon seul désir*, who resides unseen inside the tent. Exodus, the second book of the Bible, offers a very good description of worship inside the tent of meeting.

[7] Now Moses used to take a tent and pitch it outside the camp some distance away, calling it the "tent of meeting." Anyone inquiring of the Lord would go to the tent of meeting outside the camp. [8] And whenever Moses went out to the tent, all the people rose and stood at the entrances to their tents, watching Moses until he entered the tent. [9] As Moses went into the tent, the pillar of cloud would come down and stay at

the entrance, while the Lord spoke with Moses. [10] *Whenever the people saw the pillar of cloud standing at the entrance to the tent, they all stood and worshiped, each at the entrance to their tent.* [11] *The Lord would speak to Moses face to face, as one speaks to a friend. Then Moses would return to the camp, but his young aide Joshua son of Nun did not leave the tent.* (Exodus 33:7-11)

There can be no doubt that if Moses' tent of meeting had an inscription above the entrance it would be: *À mon seul désir*. The desire of Moses and Joshua's hearts was worship, i.e., being in the Lord's presence, where "the Lord would speak to Moses face to face, as one speaks to a friend." And, look at the people's response when they saw Moses and Joshua enter the tent. They worshiped too while standing at the entrance of their tents. From worshipful hearts and a people who desired to be in the Lord's presence emerged not only the nation of Israel, but a civilization of which we are heirs.

History teaches that great civilizations are built upon major battles won, abundant crops and food, science and exploration, and security to name a few. Yet victory in battle comes from courage and valor, abundant food comes from wise decisions and God's blessing, science and exploration come from curious and humble minds that are willing to accept failure and learn – a prideful mind can accept neither – and security comes from honesty, just laws, and obedience to the law. Courage, valor, wisdom, humility, honesty, justice, and obedience are virtues acquired in the tent of meeting, because all these come from God, as well as the greatest virtue of all, which is love. Therefore, great civilizations aren't ultimately built on battles won and other big things, but on small things – things inside the tent of meeting – which actually aren't small at all. Moses and Joshua, who founded and built a nation, possessed all these virtues in abundance, because they worshiped God in the tent of meeting. The Lord God was their *À mon seul désir.*

Exodus also describes another tent of meeting. In fact this tent of meeting is mentioned far more often than Moses' tent of meeting. The Tabernacle throughout the Book of Exodus is referred to as the tent of meeting. Exodus 40:2 says, "Set up the tabernacle, the tent of meeting, on the first day of the first month," and this is just one of numerous references to the Tabernacle as the tent of meeting. It can get confusing! Was the tent of meeting the small tent that Moses' pitched outside of camp, where he and Joshua worshiped in a private and personal place, or was the tent of meeting, the highly public, formal, and ceremonial-rich Tabernacle, where all the Children of Israel were called to worship God? The answer is: it was both, and this dual use of the phrase tells us today that worship of God takes place in our heart and in the church sanctuary. One should augment and enrich the other, and in both we should find our *À mon seul désir.* But many, perhaps most Westerners, do not find their *À mon seul désir* in the church sanctuary and as a result, they cannot conceive of a tent of meeting in their heart. An alternative interpretation of the Lady and the Unicorn tapestry tells us why so many Westerners today are left searching for their *À mon seul désir.*

As mentioned earlier, there is no record of what the artist was attempting to convey in the panel that shows the noble lady holding her necklace and her maidservant standing nearby with an open box. We have interpreted it as the lady removing her jewels and placing them in the box as a sign of her intention to lay aside all her worldly possessions, enter the tent of her only desire, and worship God. An alternate interpretation is that she is not removing her jewels, but in fact she is putting the necklace on. It's such a minor thing! Is she removing her jewels or putting them on? Yet the difference between the two interpretations reveals why so many Westerners go through life never finding their *À mon seul désir*, and this revelation exposes the soul of humanity.

In the first interpretation, we said that the noble lady's *À mon seul désir* was to worship God inside the tent. This is true, but we need to be more precise. The actual sole desire of every person is to be loved. The love between husband and wife, parent and child, brothers and sisters, and among friends is indeed special, meaningful, and as we have seen so vividly during this COVID pandemic, expressing that love in person, i.e., entering their tent and being with them, is essential. Yet each of these relationships, no matter how genuine the love, disappoints. We disappoint the people we love and in turn they disappoint us. Hopefully, it's not often, but we all know it happens. Therefore, person-to-person love never truly satisfies humanity's deepest *À mon seul désir,* which is to be loved unconditionally, i.e., loved for simply who we are. But even unconditional love alone is not enough to satisfy our needy human hearts. We also want a love in which we can rest, i.e., trust, let our guard down, and will not ever disappoint. Such a love only comes from God in the person of Jesus Christ. This love is humankind's *À mon seul désir*, and we are made to seek it. Such love is eternal, and therefore, only the Eternal God can satisfy this need.

In the second interpretation, where the noble lady is taking the jewels from the box, fastening them around her neck, and entering the tent, an entirely different dynamic is at work. The noble lady still seeks unconditional love in which she finds rest, but by wearing the necklace, she's saying Christ's love and the things of this world are my *À mon seul désir*. But, the Bible is clear, both cannot be your *À mon seul désir*. C.S. Lewis described the consequences of this choice by characterizing the lady's desire for the necklace as earth, and her competing desire for God as Heaven. He wrote:

I think earth, if chosen instead of Heaven, will turn out to have been, all along, only a region in Hell: and earth, if put second to Heaven, to have been from the beginning a part of Heaven itself.[39]

If the lady is putting the necklace on she is choosing the things of earth and in doing so cannot receive the treasures of heaven, e.g., unconditional love in which we find rest. Sadly, the noble lady of the tapestry is representative of so many Western men and women today. We are what the New Testament calls "worldly." In fact, we carry worldliness in our pockets and purses in the form of smart devices that connect us to the world. We may (and should) silence them when we enter the sanctuary, but we don't turn them off; not even for a second. With phones on vibrate and our minds occupied with things of the world, we enter the church sanctuary and feel nothing, experience nothing, and believe there is nothing to believe in. Worse, we enter the tent of meeting and find no one, no Savior, and no God. As a result, awareness of and belief in God, ourselves, and the West's story of Judeo-Christianity slips farther away. Our confidence is shaken and is replaced with shallow and false bravado. A verse from James in the New Testament says, "Draw near to God and he will draw near to you." (James 4:8) But, to Western men and women, God seems distant, and perhaps inconsequential to our lives. How can we draw near to God?

By placing all our worldly jewels in a box and earnestly seeking him, because the verse from James is true: "Draw near to God and he will draw near to you." We should look to churches to help, and they are helpful, because they are the keepers and conveyors of the faith. Christ is the head of the church. But, churches, like individuals, can often be more attached to her worldly jewels than they are to Christ. Near the time that the Lady and the Unicorn tapestries were woven, there were two popes – one in Rome and the other in Avignon, France. It was the time of the Great Schism in the church. Throughout the two thousand year history of Christianity, there is scarcely a time where some part of Christendom wasn't engaged in politics. The abbots of Cluny, who built the building we're in certainly welded political power and influence in Europe for centuries.

Westerners look back at church history and the current status of churches and apply a weird purity test that in a way is perfectly logical. The West is unquestionably morally depraved and church attendance is at historic lows and biblical illiteracy at historic highs. Within this upside-down context, depraved Westerners demand a pure church, a church free of scandal, and a church that adheres to the fuzzy half-baked notions they have about Jesus' love, while at the same time, they claim to be agnostics or atheists. When churches fail the West's purity test, the reaction is a morally superior, "I told you so! Those Christians are hypocrites." It's all so strangely infantile. Of course, churches should strive for righteousness and should teach and live Christ's gospel – the full gospel and not the half-baked gospel of biblical illiterates. But, mature adults understand that Christians – like all people – have moral failings and churches – like all organizations run by people – don't always do what they should. What the weird purity test actually reveals, and why it is perfectly logical, is because depraved and infantile Westerners crave unconditional love and when they can't find it, they react childishly. The reason they can't find their *A mon seul désir* in the tent of meeting is because they love the world more than they love Christ.

Unwilling to give up the things of earth, they cannot see the treasures of heaven. The beating heart of the Cluny abbots was not their Parisian townhouse. It was not their extensive library, art collection, land, and buildings. The beating heart of Cluny and the beating heart of the church today is the prayer that Cluny monks prayed during the monastery's 900 year history.

O God, by whose grace your servants the Holy Abbots of Cluny, Kindled with the flame of your love, became burning and shining lights in your Church: Grant that we also may be aflame with the spirit of love and discipline, and walk before you as children of light; through Jesus Christ our Lord, who lives and reigns with you, in the unity of the Holy Spirit, one God, now and forever.

The unconditional love and rest in Jesus Christ is the *A mon seul désir* that Western men and women seek. It is here and it has never gone away. Perhaps right now, unseen and unknown to us, the Holy Spirit is at work and Westerners are looking for their tent of meeting, and hoping to enter and worship. When we put down our worldly jewels and enter, our thirsty souls will drink Christ's living water, we will be restored as a person, and in the church sanctuary we will be restored as a people.

We've spent a long time in the exhibition room looking intently at the tapestries, and as we rise to leave, the security guard approaches. He has a quizzical expression, and says, "Qu'avez-vous vu?" (What did you see?)

We hesitate, not knowing if he will understand, but we say, "La tente de la rencontre." (The tent of meeting.)

"La tente de la rencontre?" he replies even more puzzled.

We turn to glance back at the tapestry, and answer, "Oui, monsieur, c'est à mon seul désir." (It is my only desire.)

Epilogue

Bruges, Belgium

I began this book by sharing my profound dismay while on a business trip to Manchester, England. In the Prologue, I recounted my taxi ride from the Manchester train station to my hotel. While stuck in traffic, I spotted from a distance a lovely old brownstone church. It was perched on a hilltop, and in the fading light of an early spring sunset, the rich earthen hues of the heavy stones laid by generations past told the story of a people of faith. Surely, they were a people with a commitment to future generations. Otherwise, they would not have invested in such a permanent and substantial building. They were Christians, who knew Our Savior, and because they knew Him, they knew the truth of who they were as person and a people, and they wanted that truth to endure. And, this church certainly seemed to be enduring, because the stones were clean. The church was in pristine condition, and not at all like the grime-caked facades seen on most European churches. I couldn't wait for traffic to clear and my taxi to reach the hilltop so I could catch the name of this church. You will remember, it wasn't a church at all. It was a building that had once been a church, but was now luxury condos. My heart sank.

The insides of the church had been gutted and carted off to the trash bin, and the building was transformed into something it was never intended to be. Its purpose, its *raison d'etre*, and the faith of the generations that had set the stones in place were all gone, lost, and soon to be forgotten. So, it is with all of Western civilization. Our sacred identity with Christ that defines us a person, a people, and a civilization has been hammered, pried away from us, and tossed on a trash heap.

The 21st Century demolishers of the West believe, like the condo developers who gutted the old church believe, that they are creating something better. A new heaven on earth is what they promise, where racism is no more, economic disparity is a thing of the past, male and female genders are erased, marriage is what they say it is, life begins and ends when they say it does, and Earth is finally cooling, because fossil fuels are finally banned. But, what the Western demolishers are actually creating is a society with no history, no hope, no soul, no faith, no dreams, no Savior, and populated by depraved people, who embrace lesser gods that make no sense. At least the ancient polytheistic pagans assigned powers and characteristics to their gods of wood and stone.

Leviathan inhabited the seas and churned its waters. Baal could withhold rain. Aphrodite granted beauty and sexual prowess. Isis was the motherly god of even the dead. Artemis was the goddess of the hunt and fertility. At least the pagan ancients had some imagination, but the 21st Century demolishers know only how to destroy. The condo developers had a plan to repurpose the old church building, the demolishers want to level it. No stone can be left standing. The condo developers carted out pews; the West's demolishers are carting out Christ, because he stands between them and unbridled power. And, if the civilization built on Judeo-Christianity has to be destroyed to gain such power, well so be it.

Now, we are at the core of our dilemma. As Western people, our rights, freedoms, institutions, system of justice, and even our economic system are built on a Judeo-Christian foundation. As long as the foundation is intact and robust, the demolishers are thwarted. Their vision of a utopia where rights and freedoms belong not to the people but to them, and where the prosperity earned from a person's labor is not their own but belongs to them as well, is their desire. The civilization the demolishers envision cannot – at least for now – be imposed, because it is contrary to a civilization who understands that rights come from God and the prosperity that ensues from those rights is God's gift to individuals. It does not belong to the demolishers. Therefore, Christ, who is the cornerstone of our foundational story, must be diminished until he is erased, and if that's not possible, then a false Christ, one who bears no resemblance to the Messiah of the scriptures, must be foisted on the people so we will forget who Christ really is and who we really are. And truly, the saddest and most frightening part of the demolishers plan is that they receive assistance from pastors, seminaries, and denominations.

If we are to endure as a people and civilization, it must end. Therefore, we embarked on a journey to remember and recover the songs, ceremonies, scripture, prayers, and sacraments that originate in the church sanctuary and fill every aspect of Western life. Our journey at least for this book is now complete. What I hope you've grasped is that only in Christ and only through worship can Western men and women know who we were, who we ought to be, and who we can be. And, only through Christ will the 21st Century demolishers be defeated, because it is a spiritual war that we fight, and our greatest weapon is Our Savior, whom we worship.

Through worship we are restored, and the good news is that it's happening. People are waking up. Churches though in decline still exist, and while waning, more Westerners worship and place faith in Christ than the demolishers wish to acknowledge. Therefore, there is hope! Our home will be restored, and to illustrate how and where the restoration is occurring, I will share the joy I experienced on a different business trip.

Roughly fifteen years ago, I had to make an urgent and important business trip to Brussels. The EU Parliament was debating environmental legislation that, if passed, would be detrimental to my company and the chemical industry. Misinformation, competing scientific studies with divergent conclusions, alarmist claims, and confusion surrounded this legislation, and the environmental lobby and the chemical industry that I represented were both determined that their position would prevail. Therefore, my company dispatched me to Brussels to meet with a team of lawyers and lobbyists. My job was to identify and explain the key environmental health issues and help the team craft science-based answers that – most importantly – could be easily understood by politicians. That's the hardest part of the job!

On a Saturday evening, I boarded a plane at Dulles airport and arrived in Brussels on a Sunday morning. The team's first meeting was scheduled for Monday morning at the law office. But when I arrived at my hotel, there was message waiting for me. I was to call the lead attorney as soon as possible. Once in my room, I rang his number.

He was most apologetic. When he scheduled the meeting he'd forgotten that Monday was a national holiday. He explained that Belgium had numerous holidays – so many in fact that's it's hard to keep track of them! Tomorrow was a national holiday and the law office would be closed. I asked what would be open and for suggestions on how to spend the day. He said that Bruges would be open. He described it as a quaint medieval village that was preserved in time, and easily accessible by train, even on a holiday. With one last apology, we ended the call.

The next morning, I was off to Brussel's Midi Station, and quickly on a train heading northwest out of the city and into the Flemish countryside. A tranquil patchwork of farms, fields, forests, and quiet streams passed by my window. But, the weather was miserable! It was cold, blustery, and pernicious gray clouds alternately offered mist followed by rain. Bruges is hard by the North Sea, and while I hoped the weather would improve, it only got worse. As I stepped off the train, I realized the thin jacket I had packed for the trip wasn't up to the task. I was cold! Yet once inside the ancient wall that surrounds the city, I don't remember being cold, because I realized the miserable weather was a gift. There was scarcely anyone on the streets. I had this stunningly beautiful medieval village mostly to myself, and even better, the mist that painted everything gray made it seem as if I had entered a time portal to touch and feel a bygone era. This was going to be a wonderful day!

If villages, like insects, could be captured in amber and preserved with all their glory and beauty intact, that is Bruges. The amber that sealed Bruges is the slit in the tidal river that links the city to the North Sea. The sea giveth and the sea taketh, and for centuries, beginning early in the 12th Century, the sea gave to Bruges in abundance. The medieval village sat at the crossroads of the Hanseatic League that dominated and controlled trade in northern Europe. Wool from England and Scotland created a woolen fabric industry. Grain from Normandy, wine from Gasçon, pepper and spices from Portugal, leather from Genoa, and silk from the Orient were stored in Bruges' warehouses and traded on her docks. In 1309, the city opened The Bourse, which was likely the world's first stock exchange. Merchants, manufacturers, bankers, brokers, and ship captains were rich! Bruges grew wealthier by the century, until the sea taketh. Around 1500, the tidal river that linked the city to the sea began to slit-in, sealing the city in a commercial tomb. Trade stopped; businesses and people left. Centuries and progress thankfully bypassed Bruges, giving us today a perfectly preserved sample of medieval Europe, and after a bowl of hearty Flemish stew, I was ready to explore it.

Wandering its narrow streets, strolling along its quiet canals, lingering to watch haughty swans preen on tranquil ponds, Bruges is, as the travel brochures claim, the "Venice of the North." And, of course, I sampled their famous Belgium chocolate. With my wandering near its end, I came to the church whose soaring tower can be seen from any point in the city. This is the Church of Our Lady.

Like most grand European churches, Our Lady was built in the Gothic style with flying buttress and stunning stained glass windows. She was constructed from 1270 to 1280, towards the end of the frenzied European church building period. But, it's not the outside that makes Our Lady remarkable, it's what's on the inside, and on this day, I found two remarkable things inside. One was expected; the other was entirely a surprise – and a most pleasant one!

Just inside the massive church door and tucked away to the right is Michelangelo's white marble sculpture of the Madonna and Child. Created between 1505 and '06, the Christ child is depicted as a toddler. Mary is sitting, and Jesus leans against his mother's knee, who has a protective but loving posture. As with all of Michelangelo's masterpieces, the sculpture seems alive. At any moment, I expected the Christ child to look up at his mother or perhaps scurry away as toddlers often do. Making this piece even more noteworthy is the fact that it was the only work by Michelangelo to leave the Italian peninsula during his lifetime. The purchase of the undoubtedly very expensive Madonna and Child demonstrate the great wealth of Bruges, and if you saw the 2014 movie "Monuments Men," this is the statue that the American soldiers protected from Nazi thieves near the end of World War II. As historic and beautiful as the Madonna and Child is, I was soon to find something even more remarkable, as I wandered around the church.

I have ambivalent feelings about Europe's old churches. They are grand, beautiful, historic, and I want to go in. Yet, at the same time, they are more often than not dark, musty, and a little creepy. On this cold, cloudy, and rainy day, the Church of Our Lady was certainly all these things. But, I couldn't help myself! I had to explore, and in the gloomy darkness I made my way down a side aisle and around behind the altar. Small candle lit chapels opened off to the side. The occasional wood carving of biblical scenes such as Jonah and the whale or Moses parting the Red Sea were hung on the wall. Nothing unusual here, I thought as I rounded the altar to the other side of the nave. There I stopped and stared in disbelief.

Ahead and tucked away to the side of the sanctuary was a brilliantly lit area. Carefully placed palms and ferns defined the area that was filled with folding chairs. In front of the chairs was a podium with a microphone. This was obviously where parishioners worshiped. This was a living church! It wasn't just a museum. Then, beyond the designated worship area, I spotted the most remarkable thing of all.

Standing alone at the back of the sanctuary was an office cubicle just like any plain vanilla cubicle found in offices around the world. But from this cubicle, you could see flickering lights, like from a TV. I had to investigate, and my hunch was right. It was a TV sitting on a card table with four chairs facing it. Next to the TV was a VCR that was playing a movie on a continuous loop and taped to the front of the card table was a sign written in multiple languages. While not verbatim, this is what was written on the sign:

Thank you for visiting the Church of Our Lady. We are a worshiping congregation, and invite you to join us each Sunday, as we worship Our Risen and Resurrected Lord, Jesus Christ. If you don't know Jesus, we invite you to watch this film that will explain what you need to know. If you would like more information, please contact the docent. We care about you. May God bless you and keep you.

The movie that was playing is Cru's "Jesus Film."

The Church of Our Lady on that dark and stormy day offers the perfect metaphor for who we were and what we must do, if we are to preserve Western civilization and become who we ought to be and who we can be. Outside the church doors was cold, dark, and bone-chilling rain that seemed like it would never stop. Likewise is the moral and spiritual storm stirred by Western demolishers, who seem to never stop. Inside Our Lady were treasures almost beyond comprehension. That Michelangelo could make stone seem alive is a talent that is surely granted by God, and one that Our Creator rarely dispenses. But, there is so much more associated with the Madonna and Child than one man's talent. To discover the hidden treasure, we must assess his art, as the Greek's would say – *in situ* – within the situation that created it.

The Madonna and Child, and indeed all of Michelangelo's masterpieces, were birthed by an ancient and divinely led civilization that worshiped one God. He is the God that the Apostle Paul proclaimed to the Athenians. Standing on the Aeropaus, which is a stone outcropping on the side of the Acropolis, Paul told the oh-so wise and scholarly Epicurean and Stoic philosophers the following:

"People of Athens! I see that in every way you are very religious. [23] *For as I walked around and looked carefully at your objects of worship, I even found an altar with this inscription: to an unknown god. So you are ignorant of the very thing you worship—and this is what I am going to proclaim to you.*

[24] *"The God who made the world and everything in it is the Lord of heaven and earth and does not live in temples built by human hands.* [25] *And he is not served by human hands, as if he*

needed anything. Rather, he himself gives everyone life and breath and everything else. (Acts 17: 22-25)

After telling the philosophers that God is not far away, but near, and that human beings are created in God's image, Paul said:

[29] "Therefore since we are God's offspring, we should not think that the divine being is like gold or silver or stone—an image made by human design and skill. [30] In the past God overlooked such ignorance, but now he commands all people everywhere to repent. [31] For he has set a day when he will judge the world with justice by the man he has appointed. He has given proof of this to everyone by raising him from the dead." (Acts 17:29-31)

At mention of the resurrection, the Epicureans and Stoics had heard enough. Paul was sent packing and the New Testament contains no record of a church in Athens being established. In 52 CE, the approximate date of Paul's sermon, the great scholarly minds of Athens could more easily believe that Zeus assumed the form of a swan and raped Leda, who gave birth to more gods than believe that the unseen God, who created all things, "so loved the world that he gave his one and only Son, that whoever believes in him shall not perish but have eternal life." (John 3:16) But, Athens' rejection of the gospel message wasn't the norm. By 112 CE, Pliny, the governor of the Roman province, Bithynia, which is part of modern-day Turkey, complained in a letter to Emperor Trajan about the rapid spread of Christianity. He said that Christians were "many in every period of life , on every level of society, of both sexes… in towns and villages and scattered throughout the countryside." By the middle of the 2nd Century, the Christian church was established in Lyon. How or when the gospel spread to Britannia is unknown, but in the year 314, three bishops from Britain attended a church council in southern France.

As Christianity sank into the marrow of generations of Western people, it birthed a civilization founded on the very message that Paul preached and the Athenians rejected. Christ is risen – sin and death have been conquered. From this message emerged a civilization like none other in the world. It is a Christian civilization that produced the Renaissance, a rebirth of knowledge, art, beauty, and science. The hammer and chisel in Michelangelo's hand shaped stone to produce the beauty of the Madonna and Child, and likewise, it is Christ's hand with the tools of the church and the Bible that have shaped generations of people to produce the beauty of the West. This is the context – the *in situ* – that gave the world Michelangelo and his art. And, within this fertile *in situ* of Christ came hundreds and thousands of other talented thinkers and doers generation after generation. The profound beauty, weight, and glory of Christ's hand shaping a people made Western civilization, and it's on full display in the Church of Our Lady! But, this is the past and of it we must give a full account. Fortunately, it too is on display in the church.

Beyond the Madonna and Child statue lies the nave and its recesses that I have described as dark, musty, and a little creepy. Yet this shadowy area is only one part of the broader sanctuary, where hope, forgiveness, salvation, and righteousness can be grasped. Is not this duality of the broadness and light of the sanctuary set against the darkness of small recesses the perfect description of the human heart? People are capable of such noble, selfless, loving, and sacrificial deeds, and yet at the same time, we are also capable of sinful, shameful, and dreadful deeds. Here we have the story of Creation itself. God, who created everything, declared it all good and blessed humans. Yet within his goodness and blessing, sin with all its negative consequences became the human story.

Mature, rational, and thinking people understand that the human condition, and therefore human history, is the story of sinful men and women seeking their way, making their mark, and finding their pleasures in the world that God created. What Westerners grasped is that our personal stories and the story of our civilization is set within an even broader context of God's salvation for sinful men and women. Westerners believe – or at least we once believed – that it is God, who created us, loves us, sent his Son to save us, gave us the Holy Spirit, founded the church, and gave us scripture. Therefore, we have a map (scripture), a leader (Christ), reinforcement (the church), and inspiration (the Holy Spirit) to show us how we ought to live and how we can live. This is what made the West!

Do we and by extension all of Western civilization always get it right? Of course not! We fail, and more so than our victories, our failures, which are the dark and musty corners of our hearts, make us who we are. But here's the difference between the Christian foundational story of the West, and the foundational story of non-Christian nations, we believe in a living Savior, who redeems sinners and inspires us to be better people. Westerners believe – or at least once believed – that we always have hope, and that through Christ, tomorrow can be a better day.

In fits and starts, with some movement forward followed by steps backward, the Christian West developed a civilization unlike any in the world. It is the civilization of Michelangelo, Da Vinci, Picasso, Monet, and Rembrandt. It is the civilization of Beethoven, Bach, Brahms, and the Beatles. It is the civilization of Washington, Jefferson, Lincoln, James and Dolly Madison. It is the civilization of Newton, Madame Curie, Edison, the Wright brothers, and Einstein. It is the civilization of the King James Bible, Martin Luther, Martin Luther King, and Billy Graham. And there is still more! Clara Barton, Mark

Twain, Jesse Owens, Helen Keller, Anne Frank, Booker T. Washington, Queen Elizabeth I & II, Pope John Paul II, Mother Teresa, Winston Churchill, and the list of remarkable individuals could go on and on, but we'll stop here. Further, the West is the civilization that has translated the Bible into hundreds of languages and distributed the scriptures around the world. No other nations have followed Christ's Great Commission like the West. Do we have dark, musty, and creepy parts of our history? Sure, but we have a Savior, who forgives and leads us forward, and our faith in Christ is what forged Western civilization. This is our *in situ*!

Let us embrace all that is in the Church of Our Lady – the beauty, splendor, and grandeur of a civilization that has given the world greater minds, art, music, science, medicine, and lifted more people out of poverty than any other civilization in human history. Let us not shy away from failures, but honestly seek betterment, and we can because we have a Savior who forgives and who taught us righteousness. And, let us never, never forget who is the cornerstone of Western civilization. It is Christ. Therefore, let us always worship him in spirit and in truth, and worship him alone for Christ is the light of our home!

My time in the Church of Our Lady on that rainy day was at an end. As I pushed open the heavy door, I was greeted by warm sunshine. The rain had unexpectedly stopped, and here too is part of Our Lady's metaphor: God through the Holy Spirit will come and awaken us to the evil that has and is invading the West, and with awakening comes revival, renewal, and a return of goodness, mercy, justice, and love. Therefore, we must watch, wait, pray, and worship. Most importantly, we must hope. The Apostle John in his gospel wrote:

> *The light shines in the darkness, and the darkness has not overcome it.* (John 1:5)

Here is our hope! This verse is as true today as it was two thousand years ago.

We began our journey together in a Manchester taxi. Our spirit was downcast. The church was gutted and changed into something it was never intended to be, but through stories, we remembered and were reminded of who we are as a person and a people. Our stories are now told, and our journey ends in joy. We are standing in bright sunshine outside the doors of the Church of Our Lady. Our joy comes because we know that in the sanctuary shines the light of Christ. He is the light of our home, and it is he who will restore us as a person and a people.

Scripture Cited

All scripture unless otherwise noted in the text are from the New International Version (NIV) by Zondervan®.

Introduction.
Job 19:20; Psalm 139:13-14.

Chapter 1.
Matthew 11:28-30; Matthew 11:25; Psalm 51:16-17; Romans 12:2; Hebrews 4:9-11; Genesis 3:5; Genesis 3:8; Revelation 22; Luke 9:23.

Chapter 2.
John 19: 4-5; John 18:37-38; Romans 12:2; John 1:9-13;

Chapter 3.
Acts 2:14, 17; Acts 1:4-5; Acts 2:1-4; Acts 2:36-39; Joel 2:28; Hebrews 1:3; Psalm 102; Deuteronomy 14:14-17; Acts 3:19; Acts 2:38.

Chapter 4.
Genesis 3:8-9; 1 Samuel 13:14; 1 Samuel 16:13; Psalm 139; 1 Kings 1:38-39; Matthew 5:9.

Chapter 5.
John 8:10-11.

Chapter 6.
1 Kings 8:22-56; Isaiah 57:15.

Chapter 7.
Psalm 57:6-11; Exodus 10:22; Genesis 1:28.

Chapter 8.
Mark 12:41-43; Matthew 6:3-4; Matthew 10:29; Romans 1:21-23; Genesis 25:32; Luke 15:12.

Chapter 9.
Romans 10:17; Luke 1:30, 35.

Chapter 10.
Luke 4:1-4; Deuteronomy 8:3; Romans 8:14-17; 1 Corinthians 12: 23-26; Deuteronomy 8:3.

Chapter 11.
Genesis 1:10, 28; Genesis 1: 27-28; Genesis 1:9; John 8:10-11; 1 Kings 8:32; Psalm 57:8; Mark 6:3-4; Romans 10:17; Luke 4:4; Matthew 5:13; Ephesians 4:19.

Chapter 12.
Psalm 101:1; 1 Samuel 13:14.

Chapter 13.
Psalm 110:1; Acts 2:34-35; Hebrews 1:13; Luke 11:10; Genesis 25:19; Mark 3:25; Genesis 1:27; Genesis 2:18, 22, and 24; Psalm 8:4-6; Genesis 1:28 and 2:15; Genesis 2:3; Genesis 2:16; Psalm 110:1; Psalm 110; Psalms 102; Psalms 109; Psalm 104: 3-4.

Chapter 14.
2 Peter 1:3-5; 2 Peter 2:18; 2 Peter 2:19; Acts 17:27.

Chapter 15.

Psalm 42:1-2; John 4:10; Exodus 38-40; Exodus 33:7-11; James 4:8.

Epilogue.

Acts 17: 22-25; Acts 17:29-31; Proverbs 6:16-19; John 1:5.

References and Notes

The historical information presented in each chapter is readily accessible through Web search engines. Therefore, the text is not rigorously footnoted. However, where quotes are provided, books are referenced, and in instances where search terms may not be readily apparent, references have been provided and these appear below.

---

[1] Alex Danchev, "Anselm Kiefer at the Royal Academy: cataclysmic, transformational, stupendous," The Times Higher Education. October 2, 2014; see https://www.timeshighereducation.com/features/culture/anselm-kiefer-at-the-royal-academy-cataclysmic-transformational-stupendous/2016079.article.

[2] Ibid.

[3] Barnes Foundation, "Kiefer Rodin, November 17 2017 – March 12, 2018," see https://www.barnesfoundation.org/whats-on/kiefer-rodin.

[4] Rachel Corbett, "What Rodin Taught Anselm Kiefer About Making Art in an Age of Destruction," ArtNet News, November 17, 2017; see https://news.artnet.com/art-world/anselm-kiefer-rodin-barnes-1152200.

[5] Alex Danchev, "Anselm Kiefer at the Royal Academy: cataclysmic, transformational, stupendous," The Times Higher Education. October 2, 2014; see https://www.timeshighereducation.com/features/culture/anselm-kiefer-at-the-royal-academy-cataclysmic-transformational-stupendous/2016079.article.

[6] Paul Johnson, "Modern Times, The World from the Twenties to the Nineties," Revised Ed., Harper Collins, 1992, Kindle Loc. 1112.

[7] Rod Dreher, "The Benedict Option, A Strategy for Christians in a Post-Christian Nation," Sentinel, an imprint of Penguin Random House, LLC., New York, 2017.
[8] Bruce L. Shelley, "Church History in Plain Language," 4th Ed. Thomas Nelson Publishing Nashville, 2013, p. 129-130.
[9] Maurice E. Schweitzer, Alison Wood Brooks, and Adam Galinsky, "The Organizational Apology," Harvard Business Review, September 2015; see: https://hbr.org/2015/09/the-organizational-apology.
[10] Andrew Murray, "Humility and Absolute Surrender," p. 6.
[11] Opening statement in the Nuremberg Doctors Trial by Brig. Gen. Telford Taylor, United States Army; see https://www.famous-trials.com/nuremberg/1912-doctoropen.
[12] R.N. Proctor, Racial Hygiene: Medicine Under the Nazis, Cambridge, Mass, Harvard University Press, 1988.
[13] Jeremiah A. Barondess, Medicine Against Society, Journal Amer. Med. Assoc. 276, Nov. 27, 1996.
[14] See https://en.wikipedia.org/wiki/Doctors%27_trial.
[15] See https://en.wikipedia.org/wiki/Arthur_Stace.
[16] "Why is Europe losing the will to breed?" by William Reville, The Irish Times, May 15, 2016; see: https://www.irishtimes.com/news/science/why-is-europe-losing-the-will-to-breed-1.2644169.
[17] The quote and information regarding Ann life's story can be found at: https://en.wikipedia.org/wiki/Anne_Sullivan.
[18] See https://en.wikipedia.org/wiki/Helen_Keller.
[19] A.W. Tozer, "God's Pursuit of Man," p. 76.
[20] https://en.wikipedia.org/wiki/Mayflower_Compact.
[21] https://www.evangelicalsforsocialaction.org/heroes-of-the-faith/heroes-of-the-faith-elizabeth-fry/.
[22] https://www.britannica.com/topic/Christianity/Care-for-widows-and-orphans.

[23] https://answersingenesis.org/christianity/harvard-yale-princeton-oxford-once-christian/.

[24]https://www.patheos.com/blogs/crossexamined/2016/01/yeah-but-christianity-built-universities-and-hospitals/.

[25] The Heads of the Kings of Judah; see https://joyofmuseums.com/museums/europe/france-museums/paris-museums/musee-national-du-moyen-age/masterpieces-of-the-musee-national-du-moyen-age/the-gallery-of-kings-heads/.

[26] Notre Dame's kingly niches remained empty until the 19th Century when reproductions of the statues were made and installed. The original heads that were found in 1977 are exhibited in Paris' Museum of the Middle Ages.

[27] Bruce L. Shelley,. Church History in Plain Language, p. 192.

[28] I*bid*, p. 203.

[29] See https://en.wikipedia.org/wiki/Cult_of_Reason.

[30] See https://en.wikipedia.org/wiki/Cult_of_the_Supreme_Being.

[31] This conversation is imagined based on reports from Genentech's webpage regarding the company's founders; see https://www.gene.com/about-us/leadership/our-founders. For additional information about Dr. Boyer see https://www.whatisbiotechnology.org/index.php/people/summary/Boyer.

[32] See https://www.nobelprize.org/prizes/medicine/1986/cohen/biographical/.

[33] See https://bioethicsarchive.georgetown.edu/pcsbi/history.html.

[34] See https://bioethicsarchive.georgetown.edu/pcbe/bookshelf/index.html.

[35] For more information see: https://www.history.com/news/the-assassination-of-archduke-franz-ferdinand.

[36] Paul Ham, 1913, The Eve of War, Endeavor Press, Ltd. 2013, Kindle Loc. 403.

[37] All quotes in this chapter are excerpts of the "Under God" sermon by Dr. George M. Docherty, pastor of the New York Avenue Presbyterian Church, Washington, D.C. Also known as "Abraham Lincoln's Church, this sermon was preached on Sunday, February 7, 1954. For a complete transcript of the sermon see: http://www.christianheritagemins.org/articles/UNDER%20GOD.pdf.

[38] A.W. Tozer, The Pursuit of God, p. 17.

[39] C.S. Lewis, The Great Divorce, p. ix.

CPSIA information can be obtained
at www.ICGtesting.com
Printed in the USA
LVHW100429150422
715844LV00001B/45

9 798885 310659